SHAKESPEARE

A MIDSUMMER NIGHT'S DREAM

REVIEW QUESTIONS AND ANSWERS

COLES EDITORIAL BOARD

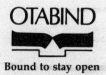

Bound to stay open

Publisher's Note

Otabind (Ota-bind). This book has been bound using the patented Otabind process. You can open this book at any page, gently run your finger down the spine, and the pages will lie flat.

ABOUT COLES NOTES

COLES NOTES have been an indispensible aid to students on fiv
continents since 1948.

COLES NOTES are available for a wide range of individual literar
works. Clear, concise explanations and insights are provided alon;
with interesting interpretations and evaluations.

Proper use of COLES NOTES will allow the student to pay greate
attention to lectures and spend less time taking notes. This wil
result in a broader understanding of the work being studied and wil
free the student for increased participation in discussions.

COLES NOTES are an invaluable aid for review and exan
preparation as well as an invitation to explore different interpretiv
paths.

COLES NOTES are written by experts in their fields. It should be
noted that any literary judgement expressed herein is just that — the
judgement of one school of thought. Interpretations that diverge
from, or totally disagree with any criticism may be equally valid.

COLES NOTES are designed to supplement the text and are no
intended as a substitute for reading the text itself. Use of the NOTES
will serve not only to clarify the work being studied, but should
enhance the reader's enjoyment of the topic.

ISBN 0-7740-3769-5

© COPYRIGHT 1997 AND PUBLISHED BY
COLES PUBLISHING COMPANY
TORONTO - CANADA
PRINTED IN CANADA

Manufactured by Webcom Limited
Cover finish: Webcom's Exclusive **DURACOAT**

CONTENTS

Page No.

PART A: The Play in Brief
INTRODUCTION.............................1
CHARACTERS IN THE PLAY 1
PART B: Questions and Answers by Act and Scene 31
PART C: General Review Questions and Answers 53

Part A: The Play in Brief

Introduction

As enjoyable and important as Shakespeare's plays are, they can be difficult to read. Since Shakespeare wrote his plays to appeal to Elizabethan audiences, much of the text is dated and means little to the average reader of today.

We are, therefore, presenting the substance of the play in readable form by eliminating, as much as possible, the outdated passages and by paraphrasing the more complicated ones. This will give you a better understanding and appreciation of the play, and will make the questions and answers more meaningful.

CHARACTERS IN THE PLAY

Theseus: Duke of Athens.

Egeus: Hermia's father.

Lysander ⎱
Demetrius ⎰ In love with Hermia.

Philostrate: Theseus' master of ceremonies.

Peter Quince: A carpenter; Prologue in the interlude.

Nick Bottom: A weaver; Pyramus in the interlude.

Francis Flute: A bellows-mender; Thisbe in the interlude.

Tom Snout: A tinker; Wall in the interlude.

Snug: A joiner; Lion in the interlude.

Robin Starveling: A tailor; Moonshine in the interlude.

Hippolyta: Queen of the Amazons.

Hermia: Egeus' daughter. In love with Lysander.

Helena: In love with Demetrius.

Oberon: King of the fairies.

Titania: Queen of the fairies.

Puck or Robin Goodfellow

Peaseblossom ⎫
Cobweb ⎪
Moth ⎬ Fairies.
Mustardseed ⎭

Other Fairies attending on Oberon and Titania.

Attendants of Theseus and Hippolyta.

[*Setting: Athens and a nearby forest.*]

ACT I

This poetic fantasy opens in the splendid palace of the legendary Greek hero, Theseus, who is the duke of Athens. Theseus and Hippolyta, his future bride, are discussing plans for their wedding, which is to take place at the next new moon. Philostrate, Theseus' master of ceremonies, and other courtiers are also present.

Theseus tells Hippolyta how impatient he is to marry her. Hippolyta assures him that:

> Four days will quickly steep themselves in night;
> Four nights will quickly dream away the time;
> And then the moon, like to a silver bow
> New-bent in heaven, shall behold the night
> Of our solemnities.

As they send Philostrate to arrange the entertainment following the marriage, Egeus appears with his daughter, Hermia, and her two suitors, Lysander and Demetrius. Hermia favors Lysander, but her father favors Demetrius. The old man is very upset by his daughter's refusal to marry the man of his choice and he has come to appeal to Theseus in the matter:

> Full of vexation come I, with complaint
> Against my child, my daughter Hermia.
> Stand forth, Demetrius. My noble lord,
> This man hath my consent to marry her.
> Stand forth, Lysander: and, my gracious duke,
> This man hath bewitch'd the bosom of my child:
> Thou, thou, Lysander, thou hast given her rhymes,
> And interchanged love-tokens with my child:
> Thou hast by moonlight at her window sung,
> With feigning voice, verses of feigning love;
> And stolen the impression of her fantasy
> With bracelets of thy hair, rings, gawds, conceits,
> Knacks, trifles, nosegays, sweetmeats, messengers
> Of strong prevailment in unharden'd youth:
> With cunning hast thou filch'd my daughter's heart;
> Turn'd her obedience, which is due to me,
> To stubborn harshness: and, my gracious duke,
> Be it so she will not here before your Grace

Consent to marry with Demetrius,
I beg the ancient privilege of Athens,
As she is mine, I may dispose of her:
Which shall be either to this gentleman
Or to her death, according to our law
Immediately provided in that case.

Theseus reminds Hermia of her duty to obey her father. Hermia asks about "the worst that may befall her" if she refuses to obey her parents' wishes. Theseus' reply is severe:

Either to die the death, or to abjure
For ever the society of men.
Therefore, fair Hermia, question your desires;
Know of your youth, examine well your blood,
Whether, if you yield not to your father's choice,
You can endure the livery of a nun;
For aye to be in shady cloister mew'd,
To live a barren sister all your life,
Chanting faint hymns to the cold fruitless moon.
Thrice-blessed they that master so their blood,
To undergo such maiden pilgrimage;
But earthlier happy is the rose distill'd,
Than that which, withering on the virgin thorn,
Grows, lives, and dies in single blessedness.

But Lysander, speaking in Hermia's defence, accuses Demetrius of having another love:

Demetrius, I'll avouch it to his head,
Made love to Nedar's daughter, Helena,
And won her soul; and she, sweet lady, dotes,
Devoutly dotes, dotes in idolatry,
Upon this spotted and inconstant man.

Theseus acknowledges that he has heard of this. Theseus and Hippolyta then leave, taking with them Demetrius and Egeus, to make further wedding plans. Lysander and Hermia, left alone, comment on their situation and the difficulties of love in general. Lysander sadly remarks:

Ay me! for aught that I could ever read,
Could ever hear by tale or history,
The course of true love never did run smooth;

Hermia suggests that they try to be patient in dealing with
their present problems:

If then true lovers have been ever cross'd,
It stands as an edict in destiny:
Then let us teach our trial patience,
Because it is a customary cross,
As due to love as thoughts and dreams and sighs,
Wishes and tears, poor fancy's followers.

But a solution to their difficulties presents itself as Lysander
tells Hermia about an aunt of his who lives far enough from
Athens to make her home a safe hideout for an eloping couple. He
suggests that they meet the next night in a forest outside Athens
and elope from there. Hermia joyfully agrees.

Their talk is interrupted by the entrance of Helena, mourning
for her lost love, Demetrius, and comparing her beauty with Hermia's:

Call you me fair? that fair again unsay.
Demetrius loves your fair: O happy fair!
Your eyes are lode-stars; and your tongue's sweet air
More tuneable than lark to shepherd's ear,
When wheat is green, when hawthorn buds appear.
Sickness is catching: O, were favour so,
Yours would I catch, fair Hermia, ere I go;
My ear should catch your voice, my eye your eye,
My tongue should catch your tongue's sweet melody.
Were the world mine, Demetrius being bated,
The rest I'ld give to be to you translated.
O, teach me how you look; and with what art
You sway the motion of Demetrius' heart!

To comfort Helena, Hermia and Lysander tell her about
their plans to elope. After they leave her, Helena comments on the
transforming power of love:

Things base and vile, holding no quantity,
Love can transpose to form and dignity:
Love looks not with the eyes, but with the mind;
And therefore is wing'd Cupid painted blind:

Helena then decides to tell Demetrius about the elopement plans, hoping that she may win Demetrius' gratitude and, more important, follow him to the woods when he pursues Hermia and Lysander.

The next scene also takes place in Athens, but we move from Theseus' palace to the world of working men. Several tradesmen—Quince, Snug, Bottom, Flute, Snout and Starveling—are preparing a play to be performed at the wedding of Theseus and Hippolyta. Quince, the director of the play, attempts to organize the group and assign parts.

Their play is the well-known story of Pyramus and Thisbe, but none of these crude fellows is familiar with it. Quince assigns Nick Bottom, the weaver, the part of Pyramus. Although Bottom would prefer to play a tyrant's role, he accepts the part of a lover, saying:

That will ask some tears in the true performing of it: if I do it, let the audience look to their eyes; I will move storms, I will condole in some measure. To the rest: yet my chief humour is for a tyrant: I could play Ercles rarely, or a part to tear a cat in, to make all split.

Flute, the bellows-mender, is to be Thisbe, but Bottom wants to play that part also:

An' I may hide my face, let me play Thisbe too, I'll speak in a monstrous little voice, 'Thisbe, Thisbe;' 'Ah Pyramus, my lover dear! thy Thisbe dear, and lady dear!'

Quince refuses. The other parts are assigned without difficulty, until Quince says that Snug, the joiner, is to have the lion's part. Bottom also wishes to play this part. Quince and Bottom argue briefly, but Quince concludes firmly:

You can play no part but Pyramus; for Pyramus is a

sweet-faced man; a proper man, as one shall see in a summer's day; a most lovely, gentleman-like man: therefore you must needs play Pyramus.

After the parts are assigned, Quince makes an appointment for the next rehearsal:

But, masters, here are your parts: and I am to entreat you, request you, and desire you, to con them by to-morrow night; and meet me in the palace wood, a mile without the town, by moonlight; there will we rehearse, for if we meet in the city, we shall be dogged with company, and our devices known. In the mean time I will draw a bill of properties, such as our play wants. I pray you, fail me not.

Bottom must still have the last word, even if he misuses it:

We will meet; and there we may rehearse most obscenely and courageously. Take pains; be perfect: adieu.

ACT II

Acts II and III and Scene 1 of Act IV take place between midnight and morning in the woods outside Athens. Act II opens with the entrance of a fairy on one side of the stage and Puck on the other. Puck asks about the fairy's activities. The fairy replies with a light and airy song:

> Over hill, over dale,
>> Thorough bush, thorough brier,
> Over park, over pale,
>> Thorough flood, thorough fire,
> I do wander every where,
> Swifter than the moon's sphere;
> And I serve the fairy queen,
> To dew her orbs upon the green.
> The cowslips tall her pensioners be:
> In their gold coats spots you see;
> Those be rubies, fairy favours,
> In those freckles live their savours:
> I must go seek some dewdrops here,
> And hang a pearl in every cowslip's ear.
> Farewell, thou lob of spirits; I'll be gone:
> Our queen and all her elves come here anon.

The fairy tells Puck that Titania, queen of the fairies, will be arriving soon. Puck warns the fairy that Oberon, the fairy king, also plans to be there shortly. Puck explains that Oberon and Titania are arguing fiercely over a changeling, a lovely boy stolen from an Indian king. Titania has made the boy her special favorite, and Oberon, who is jealous, wants the child for himself. Every time Oberon and Titania meet, Puck continues, they quarrel so violently that their elves are frightened and crawl into acorn cups to hide.

The fairy suddenly recognizes Puck as Robin Goodfellow:

> Either I mistake your shape and making quite,
> Or else you are that shrewd and knavish sprite
> Call'd Robin Goodfellow: are not you he
> That frights the maidens of the villagery;
> Skim milk, and sometimes labour in the quern,
> And bootless make the breathless housewife churn;

And sometime make the drink to bear no barm;
Mislead night-wanderers, laughing at their harm?
Those that Hobgoblin call you, and sweet Puck,
You do their work, and they shall have good luck:
Are not you he?

Puck admits that he is Robin Goodfellow and describes more
of his mischief:

Thou speak'st aright;
I am that merry wanderer of the night.
I jest to Oberon, and make him smile,
When I a fat and bean-fed horse beguile,
Neighing in likeness of a filly foal:
And sometime lurk I in a gossip's bowl,
In very likeness of a roasted crab;
And when she drinks, against her lips I bob
And on her withered dewlap pour the ale.
The wisest aunt, telling the saddest tale,
Sometime for three-foot stool mistaketh me;
Then slip I from her bum, down topples she,
And 'tailor' cries, and falls into a cough;
And then the whole quire hold their hips and laugh;
And waxen in their mirth, and neeze, and swear
A merrier hour was never wasted there.

Their discussion ends when Oberon and Titania, followed by
their fairies, appear at opposite ends of the forest. Oberon and
Titania begin to quarrel immediately. Oberon reminds her that he
is her lord, and Titania answers by reminding him that he has had
many ladies. She points out that he has only returned from India
because Hippolyta, one of his former loves, is about to be married. Oberon, in self-defence, accuses Titania of being in love with
Theseus and he then names several women whom Theseus abandoned for Titania. Titania angrily remarks that the arguing between her and Oberon has led to unpleasant weather conditions
and, as a result of this "distemperature" in nature, the seasons are
all mixed up. Oberon answers that this quarrelling between them
would be unnecessary if she would only give him the changeling.
Titania refuses to give him up, though, and she leaves with her
fairies.

Oberon decides to take drastic action against Titania. He calls Puck over and tells him:

Thou rememberest
Since once I sat upon a promontory,
And heard a mermaid, on a dolphin's back,
Uttering such dulcet and harmonious breath,
That the rude sea grew civil at her song,
And certain stars shot madly from their spheres,
To hear the sea-maid's music.

Puck: I remember.

Oberon: That very time I saw, but thou couldst not,
Flying between the cold moon and the earth,
Cupid all arm'd: a certain aim he took
At a fair vestal throned by the west,
And loosed his love-shaft smartly from his
bow,
As it should pierce a hundred thousand hearts:
But I might see young Cupid's fiery shaft
Quench'd in the chaste beams of the watery
moon,
And the imperial votaress passed on,
In maiden meditation, fancy-free.
Yet mark'd I where the bolt of Cupid fell:
It fell upon a little western flower,
Before milk-white, now purple with love's
wound,
And maidens call it love-in-idleness.
Fetch me that flower; the herb I shew'd thee
once:
The juice of it on sleeping eye-lids laid
Will make or man or woman madly dote
Upon the next live creature that it sees.
Fetch me this herb; and be thou here again
Ere the leviathan can swim a league.

Puck leaves to get the flower, and Oberon describes his plan in a soliloquy:

9

Having once this juice,
I'll watch Titania when she is asleep,
And drop the liquor of it in her eyes.
The next thing then she waking looks upon,
Be it on lion, bear, or wolf, or bull,
On meddling monkey, or on busy ape,
She shall pursue it with the soul of love:
And ere I take this charm from off her sight,
As I can take it with another herb,
I'll make her render up her page to me.
But who comes here? I am invisible;
And I will overhear their conference.

The two people approaching are Demetrius, followed by Helena. Demetrius is angry because Helena is pursuing him, and she is in despair because of his anger. As he rushes off, Helena says:

I'll follow thee, and make a heaven of hell,
To die upon the hand I love so well.

Oberon vows to help her. The return of Puck brings Oberon's attention back to his own problems. Learning that Puck has the enchanted flower, Oberon instructs him:

I pray thee, give it me.
I know a bank where the wild thyme blows,
Where oxlips and the nodding violet grows;
Quite over-canopied with luscious woodbine,
With sweet musk-roses, and with eglantine:
There sleeps Titania sometime of the night,
Lull'd in these flowers with dances and delight;
And there the snake throws her enamell'd skin,
Weed wide enough to wrap a fairy in:
And with the juice of this I'll streak her eyes,
And make her full of hateful fantasies.
Take thou some of it,

Giving Puck part of the herbs, Oberon orders him to search the woods for a man in Athenian garments, whose eyes must also be rubbed with the juice of the flower:

Seek through this grove:
A sweet Athenian lady is in love
With a disdainful youth: anoint his eyes;
But do it when the next thing he espies
May be the lady: thou shalt know the man
By the Athenian garments he hath on.
Effect it with some care that he may prove
More fond on her than she upon her love:
And look thou meet me ere the first cock crow.

In another part of the forest, Titania is being sung to sleep by her fairies:

First Fairy: You spotted snakes with double tongue,
  Thorny hedgehogs, be not seen;
Newts and blind-worms, do no wrong,
  Come not near our fairy queen.

Chorus: Philomel, with melody
  Sing in our sweet lullaby;
Lulla, lulla, lullaby, lulla, lulla, lullaby:
    Never harm,
    Nor spell, nor charm,
  Come our lovely lady nigh;
  So, good night, with lullaby.

First Fairy: Weaving spiders, come not here;
  Hence, you long-legg'd spinners, hence!
Beetles black, approach not near;
  Worm nor snail, do no offence.

While she is sleeping, Oberon appears and, sprinkling the nectar on her eyelids, casts a spell over her:

What thou seest when thou dost wake,
Do it for thy true-love take;
Love and languish for his sake:
Be it ounce, or cat, or bear,
Pard, or boar with bristled hair,
In thy eye that shall appear

When thou wakest, it is thy dear:
Wake when some vile thing is near.

Oberon leaves, and Titania continues to sleep. Lysander and Hermia soon arrive. Lysander confesses that he is lost and he suggests that they sleep there until morning. But Hermia, "for love and courtesy," will not sleep beside him:

Lie further off; in human modesty,
Such separation as may well be said
Becomes a virtuous bachelor and a maid,
So far be distant; and, good night, sweet friend:
Thy love ne'er alter till thy sweet life end!

While they are asleep at some distance from each other, Puck approaches, sees the man in Athenian garments, applies the love juice to his eyes (speaking a charm at the same time) and runs out. Suddenly, Demetrius rushes through the forest, followed, a moment later, by Helena. In their haste, neither notices Hermia. Demetrius dashes away, while Helena, "out of breath in this fond chase," pauses long enough to notice the sleeping Lysander.

Lysander wakes up and, without any warning, begins to express his love for Helena. She is overwhelmed by this sudden display of affection, and Lysander explains:

Not Hermia but Helena I love:
Who will not change a raven for a dove?
The will of man is by his reason sway'd
And reason says you are the worthier maid.
Things growing are not ripe until their season:
So I, being young, till now ripe not to reason;
And touching now the point of human skill,
Reason becomes the marshal to my will,
And leads me to your eyes; where I o'erlook
Love's stories, written in love's richest book.

But Helena thinks that this is all a joke and that the others are attempting to make fun of her. She rushes off, followed by Lysander, who says to the sleeping Hermia as he passes her:

Hermia, sleep thou there:
And never mayst thou come Lysander near!
For as a surfeit of the sweetest things
The deepest loathing to the stomach brings,
Or as the heresies that men do leave
Are hated most of those they did deceive,
So thou, my surfeit and my heresy,
Of all be hated, but the most of me!
And, all my powers, address your love and might
To honour Helen and to be her knight!

Hermia, awakened by the disturbance, thinks she has been dreaming:

Help me, Lysander, help me! do thy best
To pluck this crawling serpent from my breast!
Ay me, for pity! what a dream was here!
Lysander, look how I do quake with fear:
Methought a serpent eat my heart away,
And you sat smiling at his cruel prey.
Lysander! what, removed? Lysander! lord!
What, out of hearing? gone? no sound, no word?
Alack, where are you? speak, an if you hear;
Speak, of all loves! I swoon almost with fear.
No? then I well perceive you are not nigh:
Either death or you I'll find immediately.

ACT III

It is midnight, and the actors have come to their rehearsal. The green clearing is their stage, and the clump of hawthorn in which Titania is sleeping will be their dressing room. Since they were assigned their parts they have read the play, and there are numerous details which must be settled. Bottom points out that Pyramus must draw a sword to kill himself, an act bound to offend the ladies. Perhaps, Starveling, the tailor, suggests, the killing must be left out. But Bottom has already discovered the solution. He suggests that Starveling write a prologue explaining that Pyramus is not really dead and, further, that Pyramus is really Bottom.

Snout, the tailor, then raises the question of whether the ladies will be frightened by the lion. Bottom agrees that they must "look to't," and it is decided that Snug, who will be playing the lion, must let his face show through the lion's neck and explain to the ladies that he is not really the fierce creature he seems to be.

Quince, as the stage director, agrees to these changes. He adds, however, that there are "two hard things" still to be worked out. The first is how to arrange moonlight, since it is by moonlight that Pyramus and Thisbe meet. Quince proposes:

> . . . one must come in with a bush of thorns and a lantern, and say he comes to disfigure, or to present, the person of Moonshine.

The second problem is that they need a wall, since the lovers must speak through a crack in the wall. Bottom provides the solution for this difficulty:

> Some man or other must present Wall: and let him have some plaster, or some loam, or some rough-cast about him, to signify Wall; and let him hold his fingers thus, and through that cranny shall Pyramus and Thisbe whisper.

They finally get down to the rehearsal, just as Puck, invisible, enters. Pyramus has the first speech, after which he exits, in Quince's phrase, "to see a noise that he heard." Puck, up to his tricks, follows him out, and Bottom returns for his next line with an ass' head upon his shoulders. This sight so terrifies the others that they run away, leaving Bottom in bewilderment. Snout, who hasn't believed his eyes, returns for another look, only to be frightened away again. Then Quince also reappears to shout, "Bless thee, Bottom! bless thee! thou art translated" and he rushes off again. Bottom is entirely unaware of his transformation and is convinced they are playing a trick on him. He decides to remain where he is and sing so that the others will hear that he is not afraid.

His singing awakens Titania, who immediately falls in love with him. By the end of the second verse of Bottom's song, she declares her great passion for him:

> I pray thee, gentle mortal, sing again:
> Mine ear is much enamour'd of thy note;
> So is mine eye enthralled to thy shape;
> And thy fair virtue's force perforce doth move me
> On the first view to say, to swear, I love thee.

Bottom's reply is wiser than he knows:

> Methinks, mistress, you should have little reason for that: and yet, to say the truth, reason and love keep little company together now-a-days; the more the pity, that some honest neighbours will not make them friends.

He wants nothing but to get out of the woods, yet he allows Titania to entice him to accompany her:

> Out of this wood do not desire to go:
> Thou shalt remain here, whether thou wilt or no.
> I am a spirit of no common rate:
> The summer still doth tend upon my state;
> And I do love thee: therefore, go with me;
> I'll give thee fairies to attend on thee;
> And they shall fetch thee jewels from the deep,
> And sing, while thou on pressed flowers dost sleep:
> And I will purge thy mortal grossness so,
> That thou shalt like an airy spirit go.
> Peaseblossom! Cobweb! Moth! and Mustardseed!

Titania orders her fairies to serve Bottom and "bring him silently" to her bower.

It is now time for Puck to report to Oberon. He tells him proudly what happened to the actors and of Titania's love for Bottom. He also reports that he has rubbed the Athenian's eyes with the juice. Just then, Demetrius and Hermia come in, and Oberon exclaims, "Stand close: this is the same Athenian." Puck replies, "This is the woman, but not this the man."

They listen to Hermia as she accuses Demetrius of killing Lysander out of jealousy:

Out, dog! out, cur! thou drivest me past the bounds
Of maiden's patience. Hast thou slain him, then?
Henceforth be never number'd among men!
O, once tell true, tell true, even for my sake!
Durst thou have look'd upon him being awake,
And has thou kill'd him sleeping? O brave touch.
Could not a worm, an adder, do so much?
An adder did it; for with doubler tongue
Than thine, thou serpent, never adder stung.

Demetrius has tried to make love to her through all this but, when Hermia at last rushes away, he gives up in despair and lies down to sleep. Oberon questions Puck:

What hast thou done? thou has mistaken quite,
And laid the love-juice on some true-love's sight:
Of thy misprision must perforce ensue
Some true love turn'd, and not a false turn'd true.

Oberon tells Puck to find Helena quickly and bring her to where she can be the first person Demetrius sees on waking. Meanwhile, he puts on Demetrius' eyes the potent juice and recites another charm:

Flower of this purple dye,
Hit with Cupid's archery,
Sink in apple of his eye.
When his love he doth espy,
Let her shine as gloriously
As the Venus of the sky.

When thou wakest, if she be by,
Beg of her for remedy.

Puck returns to tell Oberon that Helena and Lysander are
approaching. Oberon cautions Puck to hide: "the noise they
make/Will cause Demetrius to awake." Puck observes:

Then will two at once woo one;
That must needs be sport alone;
And those things do best please me
That befal preposterously.

Helena, pursued by Lysander, enters. Lysander attempts to
make love to Helena, but she rejects him. Their conversation
wakes up Demetrius, who, seeing Helena, immediately expresses
his own love for her:

O Helen, goddess, nymph, perfect, divine!
To what, my love, shall I compare thine eyne?
Crystal is muddy. O, how ripe in show
Thy lips, those kissing cherries, tempting grow!
That pure congealed white, high Taurus' snow,
Fann'd with the eastern wind, turns to a crow
When thou hold'st up thy hand: O, let me kiss
This princess of pure white, this seal of bliss!

Helena is amazed. Before she was loved by no one and now
she is loved by two men. Helena is sure these young men are
playing a cruel trick on her:

O spite! O hell! I see you all are bent
To set against me for your merriment:
If you were civil and knew courtesy,
You would not do me thus much injury.
Can you not hate me, as I know you do,
But you must join in souls to mock me too?
If you were men, as men you are in show,
You would not use a gentle lady so;
To vow, and swear, and superpraise my parts,
When I am sure you hate me with your hearts.
You both are rivals, and love Hermia;

17

And now both rivals, to mock Helena:
A trim exploit, a manly enterprise,
To conjure tears up in a poor maid's eyes
With your derision! none of noble sort
Would so offend a virgin, and extort
A poor soul's patience, all to make you sport.

This speech leads Lysander to offer Demetrius Hermia in exchange for Helena. Demetrius refuses the offer just as Helena arrives. Lysander tells Hermia almost immediately that he is now in love with Helena. Hermia is shocked, and Helena is convinced that Hermia, too, is involved in the plot to humiliate her:

Injurious Hermia! most ungrateful maid!
Have you conspired, have you with these contrived
To bait me with this foul derision?
Is all the counsel that we two have shared,
The sister's vows, the hours that we have spent,
When we have chid the hasty-footed time
For parting us—O, is all forgot?
All school-days' friendship, childhood innocence?
We, Hermia, like two artificial gods,
Have with our needles created both one flower,
Both on one sampler, sitting on one cushion,
Both warbling of one song, both in one key;
As if our hands, our sides, voices, and minds,
Had been incorporate. So we grew together,
Like to a double cherry, seeming parted,
But yet an union in partition;
Two lovely berries moulded on one stem;
So, with two seeming bodies, but one heart;
Two of the first, like coats in heraldry,
Due but to one, and crowned with one crest.
And will you rent our ancient love asunder,
To join with men in scorning your poor friend?

Hermia continues to be confused. Demetrius threatens to attack Lysander, to whom Hermia clings to prevent him from striking Demetrius. Lysander, attempting to break away, calls Hermia several unflattering names and finally tells her that he hates her. Hearing Lysander declare his love for Helena, Hermia, no longer quietly bewildered, becomes angry. A bitter argument, involving all four characters, follows. Finally, Lysander and Demetrius leave to fight over Helena. Alone with Hermia, Helena says:

> I will not trust you, I
> Nor longer stay in your curst company.
> Your hands than mine are quicker for a fray,
> My legs are longer though, to run away.

Hermia also leaves, after remarking, "I am amazed, and know not what to say."

Oberon and Puck have witnessed this entire scene. Now that the lovers are gone, Oberon scolds Puck for his mistake, and Puck excuses himself:

> Believe me, king of shadows, I mistook.
> Did not you tell me I should know the man
> By the Athenian garments he had on?
> And so far blameless proves my enterprise,
> That I have 'nointed an Athenian's eyes;
> And so far am I glad it so did sort,
> And this their jangling I esteem a sport.

Oberon then orders Puck to go and lead the two men in different directions so that neither will meet the other and, when they are so weary that they lie down to sleep, to put an herb into Lysander's eye that will restore his love for Hermia. By the end of the act, Puck has carried out his directions so well that all four of the lovers are asleep on different parts of the stage and he can apply the love potion to Lysander's eyes in safety. As Puck squeezes the juice on Lysander's eyes, he chants:

> When thou wakest,
> Thou takest
> True delight
> In the sight
> Of thy former lady's eye:
> And the country proverb known,
> That every man shall take his own,
> In your waking shall be shown:

Jack shall have Jill;
Nought shall go ill;
The man shall have his mare again, and all shall be well.

ACT IV

Titania and Bottom enter, attended by fairies. Oberon also enters, but he is invisible to all except the audience. Titania speaks lovingly to Bottom:

Come, sit thee down upon this flowery bed,
 While I thy amiable cheeks do coy,
And stick musk-roses in thy sleek smooth head,
 And kiss thy fair large ears, my gentle joy.

Bottom, thoroughly enjoying himself, orders the fairies to make him more comfortable. Peaseblossom is to scratch his ears, Cobweb is to go hunting for him and Mustardseed is assigned to help scratch.

When Titania asks Bottom whether he would like music, he calls for tongs and bones. And when she asks him what he would like to eat, he answers:

Truly, a peck of provender: I could munch your good
dry oats. Methinks I have a great desire to a bottle of
hay: good hay, sweet hay, hath no fellow.

Bottom soon becomes tired and he falls asleep in Titania's arms. After ordering her fairies to leave, Titania addresses the sleeping Bottom:

So doth the woodbine the sweet honeysuckle
Gently entwist; the female ivy so
Enrings the barky fingers of the elm.
O, how I love thee! how I dote on thee!

Oberon then welcomes Puck to the scene and tells him about Titania's love for Bottom and how she cheerfully gave him the boy who was the cause of the quarrel. He is now quite ready to restore Titania to herself by administering another herb to her eyes and repeating this little charm:

Be as thou wast wont to be;
See as thou wast wont to see:
Dian's bud o'er Cupid's flower
Hath such force and blessed power.

She wakes at once and cries that she has been dreaming she was "enamour'd of an ass." Oberon points to Bottom, asleep nearby. Titania wonders how she could have loved this creature, adding, "O, how mine eyes do loathe his visage now!"

Oberon will explain everything to her later, but now he asks her to call for music to "strike more dead / Than common sleep of all these five the sense."

While Puck removes the ass' head from Bottom, the fairies begin their dance, which continues until Puck announces dawn and the fairies flee. Horns are heard as Theseus, Hippolyta, Egeus and attendants enter for the hunting. Theseus gives directions to the foresters and then talks with Hippolyta about his hounds.

Meanwhile Egeus has found the four lovers asleep, and Theseus remembers this is the day for Hermia's decision. He orders the huntsmen to wake them with their horns. When they are quite awake, Theseus demands an explanation for their present situation. Demetrius confesses that, by some hidden power, his love for Helena has returned and he no longer desires Hermia. At this news, Theseus suggests that his marriage hour also be theirs. They agree delightedly. But, as Theseus and his party leave the four alone, they find themselves confused and feeling as if they were still dreaming.

There is now only one sleeper, Bottom, left. He awakes very confused by his supposed dream. He thinks the rehearsal is still going on:

> When my cue comes, call me, and I will answer: my next is, 'Most fair Pyramus.' Heigh-ho! Peter Quince! Flute, the bellows-mender! Snout, the tinker! Starveling! God's my life, stolen hence, and left me asleep! I have had a most rare vision. I have had a dream, past the wit of man to say what dream it was: man is but an ass, if he go about to expound this dream. Methought I was— there is no man can tell what. Methought I was—and methought I had—but man is but a patched fool, if he will offer to say what methought I had. The eye of man hath not heard, the ear of man hath not seen, man's hand is not able to taste, his tongue to conceive, nor his heart to report, what my dream was. I will get Peter Quince to write a ballad of this dream: it shall be called Bottom's Dream, because it hath no bottom; and I will

sing it in the latter end of a play, before the Duke: perad-
venture, to make it the more gracious, I shall sing it at
her death.

Everyone is out of the woods by this time. The other actors,
gathered at Quince's house, are anxiously awaiting Bottom's return. No one can take his place. At the last moment he fortunately
appears, anxious to tell his story, but insisting that they continue
the preparations for their play.

ACT V

In Theseus' palace, the time has come for the celebrations following the weddings. Theseus is wondering about the unusual experiences of the lovers. When Hippolyta remarks, "'Tis strange, my Theseus, what these lovers speak of," he replies:

> More strange than true: I never may believe
> These antique fables, nor these fairy toys.
> Lovers and madmen have such seething brains,
> Such shaping fantasies, that apprehend
> More than cool reason ever comprehends.
> The lunatic, the lover and the poet
> Are of imagination all compact:
> One sees more devils than vast hell can hold,
> That is, the madman: the lover, all as frantic,
> Sees Helen's beauty in a brow of Egypt:
> The poet's eye, in a fine frenzy rolling,
> Doth glance from heaven to earth, from earth to heaven;
> And as imagination bodies forth
> The forms of things unknown, the poet's pen
> Turns them to shapes, and gives to airy nothing
> A local habitation and a name.
> Such tricks hath strong imagination,
> That, if it would but apprehend some joy,
> It comprehends some bringer of that joy;
> Or in the night, imagining some fear,
> How easy is a bush supposed a bear!

They are interrupted by the entrance of the lovers. As they all seat themselves on the stage, Theseus asks Philostrate what amusements are ready. Philostrate presents an elaborate list, which includes the play about Pyramus and Thisbe. This he does not recommend:

> A play there is, my lord, some ten words long,
> Which is as brief as I have known a play;
> But by ten words, my lord, it is too long,
> Which makes it tedious; for in all the play
> There is not one word apt, one player fitted:
> And tragical, my noble lord, it is;

For Pyramus therein doth kill himself.
Which, when I saw rehearsed, I must confess,
Made mine eyes water; but more merry tears
The passion of loud laughter never shed.

Besides this, Philostrate goes on to explain, the men who play
in it are no actors. Hippolyta adds her objections, but Theseus
wants to see the play anyway:

Our sport shall be to take what they mistake:
And what poor duty cannot do, noble respect
Takes it in might, not merit.
Where I have come, great clerks have purposed
To greet me with premeditated welcomes;
Where I have seen them shiver and look pale,
Make periods in the midst of sentences,
Throttle their practised accent in their fears,
And, in conclusion, dumbly have broke off,
Not paying me a welcome. Trust me, sweet,
Out of this silence yet I picked a welcome;
And in the modesty of fearful duty
I read as much as from the rattling tongue
Of saucy and audacious eloquence.
Love, therefore, and tongue-tied simplicity
In least speak most, to my capacity.

At this point, Philostrate announces the players, and, with a
flourish of trumpets, Quince appears as prologue. He is so flus-
tered that he hurries through the speech without pausing. Theseus
notes that, "His speech was like a tangled chain; nothing im-
paired, but all disordered."
The actors enter and line up, while the prologue, gaining
courage by their presence, describes them and the plot of the play:

Gentles, perchance you wonder at this show;
   But wonder on, till truth make all things plain.
This man is Pyramus, if you would know;
   This beauteous lady Thisbe is certain.
This man, with lime and rough-cast, doth present
   Wall, that vile Wall which did these lovers sunder;
And through Wall's chink, poor souls, they are content

To whisper. At the which let no man wonder.
This man, with lanthorn, dog, and bush of thorn,
  Presenteth Moonshine; for, if you will know,
By moonshine did these lovers think no scorn
  To meet at Ninus' tomb, there to woo.
This grisly beast, which Lion hight by name,
The trusty Thisbe, coming first by night,
Did scare away, or rather did affright;
And, as she fled, her mantle she did fall,
  Which Lion vile with bloody mouth did stain.
Anon comes Pyramus, sweet youth and tall,
  And finds his trusty Thisbe's mantle slain:
Whereat, with blade, with bloody blameful blade,
  He bravely broach'd his boiling bloody breast;
And Thisbe, tarrying in mulberry shade,
  His dagger drew, and died. For all the rest,
Let Lion, Moonshine, Wall, and lovers twain
  At large discourse, while here they do remain.

They all leave the stage, except for Wall, who remains to describe himself. Hearing the wall speak, Demetrius comments that "It is the wittiest partition that ever I heard discourse, my lord."

Then Pyramus enters:

O grim-look'd night! O night with hue so black!
  O night, which ever art when day is not!
O night, O night! alack, alack, alack,
  I fear my Thisbe's promise is forgot!
And thou, O wall, O sweet, O lovely wall,
  Thou stand'st between her father's ground and mine!
Thou wall, O wall, O sweet and lovely wall,
  Show me thy chink, to blink through with mine eyne!
                    [*Wall holds up his fingers.*]
Thanks, courteous wall: Jove shield thee well for this!
  But what see I? No Thisbe do I see.
O wicked wall, through whom I see no bliss!
  Cursed be thy stones for thus deceiving me!

Theseus remarks, "The wall, methinks, being sensible, should curse again." But Pyramus reassures him:

No, in truth, sir, he should not. 'Deceiving me' is Thisbe's cue: she is to enter now, and I am to spy her through the wall. You shall see, it will fall pat as I told you. Yonder she comes.

Then Thisbe and Pyramus indulge in a highly romantic dialogue. Their exit is followed by that of Wall:

Thus have I, Wall, my part discharged so;
And, being done, thus Wall away doth go.

Hippolyta thinks this is all silly, but Theseus defends it:

The best in this kind are but shadows; and the worst are
no worse, if imagination amend them.

Lion and Moonshine enter next. Lion speaks first, explaining to the ladies in the audience that he is not really a "lion-fell, nor else no lion's dam." Theseus approves of him as being "A very gentle beast, and of a good conscience."

But Moonshine has no such luck with his speech. He starts to tell who he is, but the spectators' comments confuse him so that he forgets his words and finally blurts out:

All that I have to say, is, to tell you that the lanthorn is
the moon; I, the man i' the moon; this thorn-bush, my
thorn-bush; and this dog, my dog.

Then tragedy enters with Thisbe. The lion roars and Thisbe rushes out, dropping her mantle, which the lion mangles before disappearing after her. Onto the empty stage strides Pyramus, full of poetic thoughts, which are soon disrupted by the sight of Thisbe's torn and bloody mantle. Pyramus recites a passionate speech and then kills himself with his sword.

After appropriate comments by the spectators, Thisbe enters to find her hero dead. At first she thinks he is asleep, but she is almost immediately disillusioned:

Asleep, my love?
    What, dead, my dove?
O Pyramus, arise!

27

Speak, speak. Quite dumb?
Dead, dead? A tomb
Must cover thy sweet eyes.
These lily lips,
This cherry nose,
These yellow cowslip cheeks,
Are gone, are gone:
Lovers, make moan:
His eyes were green as leeks.

O Sisters Three,
Come, come to me,
With hands as pale as milk;
Lay them in gore,
Since you have shore
With shears his thread of silk.
Tongue, not a word:
Come, trusty sword;
Come, blade, my breast imbrue:
And, farewell, friends;
Thus Thisbe ends:
Adieu, adieu, adieu.

After this tragic conclusion, Bottom steps forward and asks
the duke:

Will it please you to see the epilogue, or to hear a Bergomask dance between two of our company?

But Theseus chooses to sum up the situation himself:

No epilogue, I pray you; for your play needs no excuse.
Never excuse; for when the players are all dead, there
need none to be blamed. Marry, if he that writ it had
played Pyramus and hanged himself in Thisbe's garter,
it would have been a fine tragedy: and so it is, truly; and
very notably discharged. But, come, your Bergomask:
let your epilogue alone.

[*A dance.*]

The clock strikes twelve. It is almost the "fairy time" of

night, time for mortals to be in bed. Theseus and his company leave, and Puck slips in:

Now the hungry lion roars,
 And the wolf behowls the moon;
Whilst the heavy ploughman snores,
 All with weary task fordone.
Now the wasted brands do glow,
 Whilst the screech-owl, screeching loud,
Puts the wretch that lies in woe
 In remembrance of a shroud.
Now it is the time of night,
 That the graves, all gaping wide,
Every one lets forth his sprite,
 In the church-way paths to glide:
And we fairies, that do run
 By the triple Hecate's team,
From the presence of the sun,
 Following darkness like a dream,
Now are frolic: not a mouse
Shall disturb this hallow'd house:
I am sent with broom before,
To sweep the dust behind the door.

Oberon, Titania and their fairies join him in a dance and sing a song that is a charm to protect the newly married couples. Then the other fairies leave Puck alone again to speak the epilogue:

If we shadows have offended,
Think but this, and all is mended,
That you have but slumber'd here,
While these visions did appear.
And this weak and idle theme,
No more yielding but a dream,
Gentles, do not reprehend:
If you pardon, we will mend.
And, as I am an honest Puck,
If we have unearned luck
Now to scape the serpent's tongue,
We will make amends ere long;
Else the Puck a liar call:

So, good night unto you all.
Give me your hands, if we be friends,
And Robin shall restore amends.

Part B: Questions and Answers by Act and Scene

ACT I · SCENE 1

Question 1.
What approaching event is referred to in the opening lines of the play?

Answer
It appears from line 2 that the wedding of Theseus and Hippolyta is to take place in "four happy days." We shall see later that it is celebrated on the third day after the day on which the play opens.

Question 2.
Who were the Amazons, and what is the meaning of Theseus' remark, "Hippolyta, I woo'd thee with my sword?"

Answer
The Amazons were a mythical tribe of warlike women living along the northeastern shores of the Black Sea. The legend of their existence, besides representing the natural instinct in women to fight, probably arose from the warlike attitude of the savage Thracian tribes, who were accustomed to aid their husbands in battle. But the Amazons were believed to be exclusively women, who perpetuated their race by temporary alliances with the men of adjoining tribes. All daughters born to them were preserved, but their male offspring were either destroyed or sold into slavery. An early legend tells how one of the twelve labors of Hercules was his successfully securing the girdle of their queen, whose name was Hippolyta. This legend may account for her being confused with the later queen, Antiope. In their later history, Theseus made war on them, defeated them and carried off their queen, Antiope. Then, in turn, they attacked Athens and were driven off by Theseus, who kept their queen and married her. It is this marriage with Hippolyta or Antiope that is celebrated in the play.

Question 3.

How is Theseus' royal dignity, Hermia's determination and Lysander's scornfulness made apparent in this scene?

Answer

Theseus' love for Hippolyta is dignified, rather than passionate. He recalls his warrior days and looks forward to a ceremony of splendor and majesty. He attempts to persuade Hermia to obey her father's will but, though his sympathies are clearly with the daughter, he shows a royal respect for the dignity of law and authority.

Hermia expresses her determination to die rather than give up her lover, with whom she promises to escape, far from "the sharp Athenian law."

Lysander's scornfulness is exhibited in the contemptuous manner in which he speaks to Egeus and in his openly expressed opinion of his faithless rival, Demetrius.

Question 4.

What purpose does the opening scene serve?

Answer

We are introduced to two of the groups essential to the machinery of the play: Theseus and Hippolyta, whose coming marriage provides the framework for the action, and the lovers, who provide much of the action itself. Hermia's dilemma, having to choose between marriage to a man she doesn't love and confinement in a convent, prepares us for the shift from the court to the woods. Helena's determination to inform Demetrius of Hermia and Lysander's elopement is the complicating factor. Thus, it is arranged for both pairs of lovers to be in the woods.

Question 5.

Explain the following passage, with reference to its context.

With cunning hast thou filch'd my
daughter's heart.

Answer

Egeus, the stern father of Hermia, has given his consent to Demetrius to marry his daughter. Unfortunately for the success of his plans, she falls in love with Lysander and refuses to wed the man of her father's choice. The Athenian law was severe against disobedient daughters, and Egeus carries his complaint to the duke, accusing Lysander of having "bewitch'd the bosom of his child," and "stolen the impression of her fantasy." Egeus begs that the extreme penalty of the law be enforced against her. To filch (to steal) is generally applied to articles of small value. It is appropriately used here in loose connection with the "knacks, trifles, nosegays, sweetmeats," with which Lysander stole Hermia's heart.

Question 6.

Why does Shakespeare include the scene between Egeus and Theseus?

Answer

The scene between Egeus and Theseus establishes, among other things, Theseus' character, which serves as a touchstone for the action that later takes place in the woods. Noble, intelligent, yet aware of practical matters and knowledgeable in the law, he urges Hermia to follow a sensible course. Yet his common sense does not make him a dull clod; his speeches are among the most noble in the play. Theseus' words to Hermia anticipate his speech in the last act on the lover, the lunatic and the poet. He does not believe that such emotions as love are necessarily "true."

Question 7.

What aspects of this opening scene may be considered improbable?

Answer

Both Theseus' departure with Egeus and Demetrius, leaving the lovers alone, and Helena's decision to tell Demetrius the eloping couple's plans, a betrayal of her own interests, seem hardly credible. But Shakespeare was not concerned with reality. Indeed, one aspect of the play is the recognition of pretending, of make-believe. This is, after all, a midsummer night's *dream*.

Question 8.

Are Lysander's remarks about love echoed in any other Shakespearean play?

Answer

Lysander's words about the course of true love suggest *Romeo and Juliet*, which was probably written just before this play. Hermia's response, "If then true lovers have been ever crossed"—further recalls those "star-crossed lovers." Lysander's comparison of love to lightning,

> That, in a spleen, unfolds both heaven and earth,
> And ere a man hath power to say "Behold!"
> The jaws of darkness do devour it up—

is an echo of Juliet's anxious feelings about her love:

> It is too rash, too unadvised, too sudden,
> Too like the lightning, which doth cease to be
> Ere one can say "It lightens."

Question 9.

What is the point of Lysander's comment that "The course of true love never did run smooth?"

Answer

Lysander's and Hermia's remarks relate specifically to one of the play's main concerns—that of love. The play celebrates Theseus' marriage to Hippolyta, and much of the action presents the misfortunes of lovers. Lysander's words later in the same scene, describing love as "Swift as a shadow, short as any dream,/Brief as the lightning in the collied night" and concluding with "So quick bright things come to confusion," besides giving, for an instant, a tragic vision of what, taken in a different spirit, the woes of Hermia and Lysander might have been, tends to reduce the seriousness of their difficulties. Lovers have always had their troubles. The only thing to do, as Hermia says, is to let these sad love tales teach them patience. Lysander's words, then, anticipate the trials that are to come and indicate a comic, rather than a tragic, ending to them.

Question 10.

Comment on the poetic form of this scene.

Answer

The first part of the scene is entirely in blank verse, the dominant form of Shakespeare's drama. In the second part we find three distinct forms. Lysander clings to blank verse, except in his short description of the moon as he tells Helena about the proposed elopement. The two girls, under the sway of their emotions, express themselves in the more lyrical rhymed verse. The third form appears twice in the artificial interchange of single lines, first between Hermia and Lysander, and second, between Hermia and Helena.

The name given to this kind of responsive chant is antiphon or antiphony. Its very common use in Greek tragedy reminds the audience of the Greek setting of the play. Artificiality and rhyme are in keeping with the purpose of the play as a masque. The love stories are ridiculous, and there is no effort on the part of the author to make them realistic. In an ordinary play, he would arouse our sympathies in sincere expressions of grief and passion when the lovers find themselves alone.

ACT I · SCENE 2

Question 1.

Explain what an interlude is.

Answer

An interlude is a play performed during the intervals of a banquet or festival. Thus, the term is correctly applied to the representation of *Pyramus and Thisbe*, which is to be performed during the celebration of the duke's marriage, between "after-supper and bed-time."

Question 2.

Briefly outline the story of Pyramus and Thisbe.

Answer

Pyramus and Thisbe were two lovers who lived in adjoining houses in Babylon. Because their parents would not agree to their marriage, they used to converse secretly through the cracks in the wall that separated their fathers' gardens. On one occasion, they arranged a meeting at the tomb of Ninus. Thisbe, arriving first at the appointed spot, saw a lion and fled. In her flight, she dropped her cloak, which the lion soiled with blood from an ox he had recently killed. Pyramus, arriving shortly after and seeing the bloodstained garment, imagined that Thisbe had been murdered and, out of grief, he stabbed himself under a mulberry tree, the fruit of which was, from then on, as red as blood. Then Thisbe returned and, seeing the dead body of her lover, killed herself with his sword.

Question 3.
Explain Bottom's references to "a tyrant" and to "Ercles."

Answer
These expressions of Bottom's recall the early mystery plays, which had not quite gone out of fashion, even in the reign of Queen Elizabeth. In such plays, the tyrant was a popular part, usually assigned to a powerful actor, who would thrill the audience with his violence and melodramatic style. In other words, the tyrant's was "a part to tear a cat in; to make all split." The parts of Hercules and of Herod, like that of the tyrant, would allow a loud-mouthed, energetic actor to display his crude abilities before an ignorant, admiring audience.

Question 4.
Briefly state the purpose of this scene.

Answer
The first scene introduces the court and the lovers; this scene introduces the "rude mechanicals." We learn of their plan to meet in the woods the next night to rehearse their wedding play. We also become acquainted with Bottom, destined to become the object of Titania's love.

Question 5.
Comment on the significance of Bottom's name.

Answer
The name, Bottom, was appropriate for a weaver, for one meaning of bottom was a silkworm's cocoon. Incidentally, the more obvious association (when Bottom is topped with an ass' head) meaning, "the sitting part of a man, the posteriors," is not recorded in the Oxford English Dictionary before 1794. It may, nevertheless, have been familiar to Shakespeare's audience, for

such meanings grow in the spoken language long before they come into print.

ACT II · SCENE 1

Question 1.

Explain the expression, "mermaid on a dolphin's back" and the reference to stars "shot madly from their spheres."

Answer

The mermaid probably refers to Mary Queen of Scots, who married the Dauphin of France, represented by the dolphin. The stars are some of the English nobles who fell in her cause.

Another theory finds in Oberon's description a reference to the festivities that took place at Kenilworth, when Elizabeth paid her visit to the Earl of Leicester in 1575. According to this explanation, the mermaid and dolphin recall certain features of the pageant that formed part of the festivities, while the stars are the fireworks that accompanied the entertainment.

Question 2.

How is the story of Daphne and Apollo, referred to in this scene, relevant to the play?

Answer

Daphne was an extremely beautiful maiden, who was loved by Apollo. She rejected him and, when he pursued her and was on the point of overtaking her, she prayed to the gods for aid and was changed by them into a laurel leaf. In the play, the story is changed in that it is Apollo—or Demetrius—who vanishes and escapes his pursuer's passionate love.

Question 3.

Explain the following passage:

Why art thou here,
Come from the farthest steppe of India?

Answer

These words are addressed by Titania to Oberon during their first meeting in the woods. Inspired by jealousy, each accuses the other of infidelity. Titania suggests that the charms of Hippolyta have attracted Oberon from "the farthest steppe of India," while Oberon retaliates by commenting on her love for Theseus.

Question 4.
What are the reasons for Puck's mischievous b[...]

Answer
Robin Goodfellow is the proper name of the chara[...] referred to in the old copies of the play as Robin, or Puck. Puck,
"the patron saint of skylarking," was the general name for a
minor order of evil spirits, similar to sprites or goblins. Shakespeare makes Puck merely mischievous, not evil. In this scene, the
roguish Puck boasts of his tricks in order to prepare the audience
for the tricks he plays later on.

Question 5.
How is nature portrayed in this scene?

Answer
Nature, a very important element in the play, is brought in
largely through word painting, of which this scene presents the
first extended example. Note, in particular, Titania's discussion
of the chaotic seasons, her description of the adoption of the
mortal child and Oberon's concluding words about Titania's
sleeping place. Often, the imagery of nature is given human characteristics, such as when "the green corn/Hath rotted ere his
youth attained a beard" and "Hoary-headed frosts/Fall in the
fresh lap of the crimson rose."

Question 6.
Are there any tragic overtones suggested in this scene or in
the play in general?

Answer
There are several suggestions of troublesome or tragic conse-
quences, quickly brushed aside by the gaiety of make-believe and
the movement toward the happy ending. The hint of tragedy
appears in the resemblances and allusions in the play, and especially in the Pyramus and Thisbe story to *Romeo and Juliet*.

A different association seems to be made in this scene. When
Demetrius threatens to do Helena "mischief in the wood," where
she has come at night "with the rich worth of your virginity," the
Elizabethans, aware of holiday activities, would have thought of
the May games, described in Philip Stubbes' widely read *Anato-*

e of Abuses, where he reports that, "of forty, three-score, or a hundred maids going to the wood over night, there have scarcely the third part of them returned home undefiled." The wanderings of the assorted lovers in the later scenes and Hermia's insistence that Lysander:

> Lie further off; in human modesty,
> Such separation as may well be said
> Becomes a virtuous bachelor and a maid.

must have inspired such thoughts.

Question 7.

What evidence does this scene offer about the date of the play?

Answer

Titania's long description of a summer in which it rained nearly every day and ruined the harvest, found in lines 88-114, is an almost exact account of the summer of 1594. Since such an unnatural summer would be a matter of speculation at the time, it is supposed that the play was written immediately after it, the author adding to the interest by attributing it to a quarrel between the fairy king and queen, showing their part in human affairs.

Question 8.

What historical reference is contained in Oberon's tale of Cupid's arrow?

Answer

Oberon's story of Cupid's misdirected arrow, lines 144-168, possibly refers to the entertainment given by Leicester for Queen Elizabeth at Kenilworth castle in 1576 and his ambition to win the queen in marriage. Kenilworth was near Shakespeare's boyhood home, and he may have seen the mermaid on the dolphin's back during a display of fireworks as part of the entertainment.

ACT II · SCENE 2

Question 1.

How is the small size and swift motion of the fairies indicated in this scene?

Answer

They wear coats made of the wings of bats, a.
with which they are at constant war are such sma
musk rose cankers, weaving spiders, beetles, worm.
For them, "a third part of a minute" is enough time
many duties.

Question 2.

How is the conflict between reason and love illustrated in this scene?

Answer

A Midsummer Night's Dream is occupied almost entirely with the subject of love, and, since the play is a comedy, this theme is treated lightly. Cupid is represented as a blind and irresponsible boy, and the lovers in the play are shown as fickle and flighty, so that, even when they appear to themselves most reasonable, we may generally assume that there is little reason in their actions. Bottom speaks the truth about the lovers when he says, "reason and love keep little company together now-a-days."

ACT III · SCENE 1

Question 1.

How are the human and fairy elements of the play connected in this scene?

Answer

The workmen happen to choose for their rehearsal spot that part of the forest in which the fairy queen is sleeping, her eyes brushed with the magic juice. Puck happens to discover the actors as their rehearsal is in progress and he immediately recognizes an opportunity to follow Oberon's plan. After Puck works his mischief, the beautiful and delicate queen of the fairies becomes infatuated with "the soul of love," the "shallowest thick-skin" of them all, and the fairy element of the play thus becomes closely linked with the human.

Question 2.

Does Bottom seem comfortable in his new situation?

Answer

Most humans would feel somewhat confused at suddenly finding themselves loved by such a beautiful being as Titania or at being served by such delicate creatures as her fairies. Not Bottom, however. He is far too dull and conceited to see anything unusual in all this. Of course, he does not know that he is wearing an ass' head any more than he is aware of his personality resemblance to that particularly stupid animal. He has always taken himself seriously and he feels that he is now, at last, receiving the attention and respect he deserves. Therefore, he acts accordingly and is proud and conceited, probably believing that he is playing the part of a gracious lord dealing with loving and dutiful subjects.

Question 3.

Why does Titania speak in verse, while Bottom uses only prose?

Answer

Verse is consistent with Titania's character, since she is a poetical being. Bottom is crude and uneducated and, therefore, he uses prose. Titania's speech is full of poetic fancies and delicate imagery, while Bottom's is commonplace and coarse.

Question 4.

What do we learn about Bottom's character in this scene?

Answer

After Bottom's ridiculous singing, his dull, literal-minded attitude is further revealed in his question, "Who would set his wit to so foolish a bird?" Bottom is literal, also, in his comments on the fairies. He says he'll call on Cobweb if he cuts his finger, cobwebs being used, in those days, to absorb blood from a cut. To Mustardseed he says, "Your kindred hath made my eyes water ere now." Bottom's simple common sense and his plain humanity do not desert him when he wears the ass' head.

ACT III · SCENE 2

Question 1.

Why does Helena think that Hermia is part of a plot to embarrass her?

Answer

Helena is aware of the love that Lysander had, until now, felt for Hermia and, when he, in Hermia's presence, extravagantly praises Helena and scorns his former love, she thinks that they have agreed to make fun of her.

Question 2.

How is Helena's gentle nature revealed in this scene?

Answer

Even when most upset, Helena shows a gentle disposition, appealing frequently to the kindness and courtesy of her supposed enemies. She almost apologizes for losing her patience with them. She begs and humbles herself before them, and pleads with Demetrius and Lysander to protect her from Hermia. She distrusts herself and sees no other remedy for her distress than "death or absence." She declares that she is no match for Hermia, "though she be but little" and, on being left alone with Hermia, runs for safety.

Question 3.

Briefly contrast the quarrels of the mortals with those of the fairies.

Answer

The fairy king and queen show an evident desire to avoid violent or noisy quarrelling. They dislike anything that is ugly and unpleasant or that might interfere with their enjoyment of life. The mortals, on the contrary, give way to their natural instincts. They are passionate and unrestrained, forgetful of themselves and of how they are treating one another.

Question 4.

In this scene, Helena and Hermia seem to change places. Why is such a role reversal an effective device for comedy?

Answer

By having the heroines change places, Shakespeare satisfies our sense of justice—Helena has her day too—and keeps us from taking the troubles of either heroine too seriously. In addition, the humor of the situation is increased, for Helena suspects Hermia of having planned the whole incident. Loved at last, she thinks she is being mocked. The audience, aware of the entire situation and knowing it will end happily, is able to share Puck's amusement.

Question 5.

Are the personalities of each of the four lovers clearly defined?

Answer

The two men, Demetrius and Lysander, are not given distinctive personalities. Each is placed under the spell of the love potion and left largely as the surface picture of the romantic lover of a midsummer dream. The girls, who are not subjected to the love flower, are somewhat more defined. Hermia is dark and short, Helena blond and tall. But their differences go beyond the physical. Hermia is direct and strong-willed. Helena declares, "She was a vixen when she went to school, / And though she be but little, she is fierce." On the other hand, Helena is a timid creature, crying to the men, "I pray you . . . Let her not hurt me . . . /My legs are longer, though, to run away."

Question 6.

Show that sleep plays an important part in the action of the play.

Answer

The power of the fairies over the emotions or actions of the mortals works, for the most part, through the medium of dreams or it is exercised upon the different persons while they are in a state of unconsciousness. The changes of affection that form the principal steps in the complication and in the unravelling of the plot are all brought about by the application of the juice of the magic flowers to the eyes of the sleeping beings. This feature of the play is consistent with the dreamlike character of the whole performance.

Question 7.

In what ways can Puck be compared to the classical god, Cupid?

Answer

Puck pities the beautiful Hermia when she enters the scene "curst and sad" and, in his moment of seriousness, he thinks about the god of love.

Cupid is a knavish lad,
Thus to make poor females mad

Yet, he himself, as Oberon's agent, has been indulging in just those same cruel tricks played upon mortals that he here seems to condemn Cupid for practising.

Question 8.

Explain the following quotation: "How low am I, thou painted maypole?"

Answer

Helena is naturally upset about being made, as she imagines, an object of ridicule by her former friends. Her anger is especially directed against Hermia, whom she accuses of a lack of modesty and maiden shame, and whom she finally addresses as "you counterfeit, you puppet, you." The term, "puppet," containing a reference to her smallness, evidently offends Hermia's vanity, and she retaliates with the words of the quotation and continues,

How low am I? I am not yet so low
But that my nails can reach unto thine eyes

The expression, "painted maypole" is intended to suggest an exaggerated impression of Helena's height and to criticize her pink and white complexion. Maypoles, painted in stripes of different colors, were common objects in many villages of Elizabethan England.

Question 9.
What is the significance of Oberon's explanation of ghosts?

Answer
Oberon's explanation of ghosts has nothing to do with the action or progress of the play. It is included to make clear to an ignorant and wondering audience the difference between fairies and ghosts and to explain why the former may still be encountered in daytime.

ACT IV · SCENE 1

Question 1.
How does Bottom confuse his two natures?

Answer
He talks sometimes as an ass, sometimes as a man and sometimes as a mixture of both. He thinks at the same time of honeybags and thistles, and of the charms of music and good dry oats or sweet hay.

Question 2.
What is "the rite of May"?

Answer
Shakespeare is not referring to any ancient classical custom, but to an English custom belonging to his own age. On the first of May, young men and maidens rose very early in the morning and walked to some neighboring woods, where they decorated themselves with flowers. They would return home at sunrise with their flowers, decorate their houses and spend the remainder of the day dancing and celebrating.

Question 3.
What indications are there in this scene that the actions of the drama should not be considered in realistic terms?

Answer
The actions of the play are symbolic rather than realistic. Shakespeare frequently reminds us of the dreamlike character of the incidents and actions. The lovers are to think "no more of this night's accidents, but as the fierce vexation of a dream." Demetrius (awake) seems to feel that he is still sleeping and dreaming and he speaks of recalling his dreams. Even Bottom half confesses that he has been, in a dream, what he really is in his own nature—metaphorically an ass.

Question 4.
State the purpose of this scene.

Answer
The lovers having been sorted out, the quarrel of Titania and

47

Oberon is now settled, and Theseus and Hippolyta come to unite all the lovers in one ceremony. With Bottom restored to his former self, everything is ready for the concluding festivities.

Question 5.

How does the misuse of words (malapropism) add to the comic effect in this scene?

Answer

Bottom's remark, "I have an exposition of sleep come upon me," misuses the word, "disposition," yet he has substituted a word that is appropriate in a different, comical sense. In the next scene, Quince calls Bottom a "paramour" and Flute tells him he should have said "paragon." Again, the misused word is appropriate in a comical sense.

ACT IV · SCENE 2

Question 1.

Explain the remark, "Sixpence a day in Pyramus, or nothing."

Answer

This means that Bottom should receive a pension of sixpence a day if he plays the part of Pyramus for the duke. This is the opinion of Flute, the bellows-mender, and this opinion would, no doubt, be shared by the rest of the Athenian craftsmen, all of whom show the greatest possible appreciation of Bottom's gifts as an actor. The passage may contain a reference to some actor, which would probably be understood by Shakespeare's contemporaries, but which has now been lost. Thirty years earlier than the composition of this play, in 1564, Preston, the author of *Cambyses*, had received from Queen Elizabeth a pension of somewhat more than a shilling a day for his abilities on the stage.

Question 2.

Discuss Bottom's function and importance in the play.

Answer

Bottom's comrades miss him at the rehearsal. Flute declares, "If he come not, then the play is marred." Among his fellow actors, Bottom is assured and eager, ready to handle any situation but not domineering, simple and at ease but one of the group. Among the fairies, Bottom is equally at home, reducing them to a more ordinary nature with his practical remarks about Cobweb and Mustardseed. In good fellowship, he puts out his hand: "Give me your neaf, Monsieur Mustardseed." Bottom is, indeed, the only human to whom the fairies are visible, and he treats them precisely as he does all others, with calm and steady common sense. Even as an ass, he remains the most real—the least imaginative, if you will, but by the same token the least imaginary—of the group. His substantial nature contrasts with the fancy of the fairies and the lovers' confusion and final lift to grace. In the entire comedy, as well as in *Pyramus and Thisbe*, if Bottom "come not, then the play is marred." He thus ties together the various levels of the play.

ACT V · SCENE 1

Question 1.

In what sense does the interlude present a strong contrast to the rest of the play?

Answer

In its lack of imagination and grace, this farcical interlude presents a contrast to the delicate and beautiful movement characteristic of the fairies. The interlude is clumsy and unimaginative compared to the light, airy and fanciful fairy world.

Question 2.

Explain the meaning of the following passage:

When I have come, great clerks
   have purposed
To greet me with premeditated
   welcomes.

Answer

Theseus has decided to hear the play prepared in his honor by the laboring men of Athens. Hippolyta objects, but Theseus, being more open-minded than his wife, points out that the motives of the actors should be taken into account. He compares the good-natured attempts of the actors with those of great scholars, whose elaborate speeches of welcome often don't achieve their intended effect, owing to the nervousness of the speaker. Even in these cases, he says:

I read as much as from the rattling tongue
Of saucy and audacious eloquence.

In the passage about "premeditated welcomes," there is probably a reference to the formal addresses that were made to Elizabeth at the gates of the principal towns she visited in her progress through the country.

Question 3.

How does Puck's concluding speech resemble an epilogue?

Answer

It resembles an epilogue in that it is spoken, not in Puck's own character as a fairy to another fairy, but rather in an impersonal character on behalf of all the actors and in that it is addressed to the audience and is explanatory and apologetic. It is comparable to the epilogues in *The Tempest* and in *Henry V*.

Question 4.

Describe the reactions of the various members of the audience to the interlude.

Answer

Philostrate objects to its performance as unworthy of the attention of the duke and duchess, but he makes no comments during its performance. Hippolyta ridicules it. Theseus praises the motives of the players and overlooks their faults, appreciating the humorous situations they develop. Demetrius and Lysander try to make humorous criticisms, chiefly in puns.

Question 5.

We have already seen *Pyramus and Thisbe* in rehearsal. How does Shakespeare manage to sustain dramatic interest while presenting it again?

Answer

The dramatic interest lies in watching others watch the play. It is the reactions of Theseus and the court that concern us, for the comments of the spectators and the explanations of the amateur performers are much more significant or amusing than their play.

Question 6.

What does Theseus mean when he says, referring to the interlude, that "the best in this kind are but shadows, and the worst are no worse, if imagination amend them?"

Answer

Theseus is saying very much what Shakespeare is saying in the play as a whole: the best dramatic presentation is still just illusion. Puck, at the end, says, "If we *shadows* have offended," making Theseus himself but a shadow. He is only an actor playing a part. Bottom and his company, when they are playing *Pyramus and Thisbe*, are also shadows and no worse, in that sense, than the best of actors, if imagination "amend them" and if the audience provide with their imagination what the actors fail to provide through their acting.

Question 7.
What is Shakespeare satirizing in the interlude?

Answer
Shakespeare satirizes the extravagance and unnaturalness of popular tragedies of his day in the ridiculous language he puts into the mouths of the clowns in their play. This satire is evident in the strained alliterations—"with blade, with bloody blameful blade, he broach'd his boiling bloody breast"; with padded lines—"that I am that same wall; the truth is so"; bad rhyming—"plain" with "certain," "sinister" with "whisper," "pap" with "hop"; repetitions—"crannied hole or chink"; excessive use of classical references—"Leander, Helen, Procris, Cophalus"; and absurd transferred adjectives—"finds his trusty Thisbe's mantle slain," "blameful blade" and "boiling breast."

Part C: General Review Questions and Answers

Question 1.
Discuss the three worlds of the play.

Answer
The four lovers inhabit one of the worlds of the play. Their situation is that of a typical, frustrated romance, with the father demanding that his daughter marry a man she doesn't love. The situation also includes a lovesick maiden who has been abandoned by this same man. Although this situation contains the ingredients of tragedy, we see that it is treated in a lighter, comic vein. Rather than displaying great passion and emotional stress, the speeches are so stylized and formal that what we observe are the typical young lovers in the typical romance. As a result, we are kept from feeling the deeper, stronger, more tragic emotions that are potentially present. When the lovers' confusion is at its height in the woods, they do break out of their customary wooden roles and exhibit some true feeling. This is more true of the girls than of their boyfriends, who continue to be rather shallow.

Another world in this play is occupied by the Athenian workmen. These characters are very different from the above. In contrast to the formal poetry that the lovers speak, these simple men speak the prose of comic realism. Their situation is also contrasted with that of the lovers. The lovers are misled by illusion in the form of Puck's mischief with the love juice. The workmen attempt to deal with illusion in the form of a play they produce for Theseus' wedding. We are shown their rehearsal, which displays the great pains they take to explain away every illusion. To these men, reality and illusion are two entirely separate notions, and they insist upon stating which is which at every point where the slightest confusion might arise. They take absolutely no chances on this question. The manner in which their production progresses is a classic expression of the position they represent on the reality-illusion question—a question at the heart of this play. When Bottom and his fellow actors deal with the moon, even that is brought down to earth and made to conform to their no-nonsense realism. Better have one of their own company represent the moon than leave the matter up to that shifting natural phenomenon. Of course, with the transformation of Bottom himself, this world enters the play's general confusion of reality and illusion. But Bottom is able to resolve this into a genuine union.

We witness yet a third world in this play in the fairy kingdom, ruled by Oberon and Titania. This world is Shakespeare's own creation. His fairies differ from those of folk tradition with respect to size, nature and activity. They are small, kindly and associated with flowers. Oberon and Titania speak beautiful poetry. Puck's poetry is remarkable for an energy and roughness all its own. Puck is Oberon's lieutenant. His character and the poetry he speaks expressing it contrast with the delicate, airy fairies and their lyric verses. When the lovers enter the fairy world, their wooden, uninteresting speeches contrast with the flexibility and grace of speech in this other world.

Question 2.
How are the separate worlds of the play connected?

Answer
Although the workmen and the lovers are very different, connections are established between the two groups as soon as we meet the second. Later, the fairies have a great deal to do with both groups. Finally all three groups come together at the court of Duke Theseus: the lovers are married, the workmen perform, and the fairies bless the household when everyone is asleep.

When we first meet the workmen, connections between them and the lovers we have already met are easily established. The reason these men are preparing a play is to entertain at that same wedding of Theseus and Hippolyta discussed in Scene 1, at which Hermia must announce her decision. The subject of the play they have chosen, while comically distant from their own world, is relevant to Hermia's predicament. Their plan to rehearse the next night in the duke's forest brings them into the same geographical area as the lovers, who also plan to meet there. When Oberon overhears Helena pleading for Demetrius' love, the king of fairies decides to help, and this begins his interference in the lovers' world. The fairy world and that of the lovers interweave extensively when Puck mistakes Lysander for Demetrius, an error that leads to many complications. The mischievous Robin involves the workmen in his world of moonlight and magic by placing an ass' head on Bottom. Thus transformed, this down-to-earth working man becomes the intimate companion of Titania, queen of fairyland. Thus, the power of fairy magic affects all three worlds, and this is a uniting force in the play. It binds together the separate strands that are destined to come together in Theseus' marriage. In short, what we have in *A Midsummer Night's Dream* is a plot structure in which the marriage of Theseus and Hippolyta is the framing event in the daylight world. It is the first thing we hear of and the last thing that happens, but the pattern that is woven within this frame is of Oberon's design. He and his assistant, Puck, take control within the framework of Theseus' marriage.

Question 3.
Justify the title of the play.

Answer
The title, *A Midsummer Night's Dream*, would suggest to an Elizabethan audience the impression of a play in which the playwright would wish to free himself from the conventional rules of drama. Midsummer night, or St. John the Baptist's Day (June 24th), was, in Shakespeare's time, popularly associated with many superstitions of a fantastic nature, so that "midsummer madness" or "such stuff as dreams are made of" are expressions that appropriately describe the sort of entertainment promised in the title to the play.

Not only do dreams play a most important part in the action of the play, but the fairy characters themselves are a sort of personified dream. Their home is in the far east, the land of dreams and enchantment. Twilight and darkness or the glimmer of a "dead and drowsy fire" draw them from their retreats and make them "frolic." At such times, they weave their plots "no more yielding but a dream." The plot of the play is thin and it is not weighed down by the conditions of outward fact and reality. Mortals and immortals, courtiers and clowns, animals and even insects and flowers play their parts in it and are associated with one another in impossible and fantastic combinations. A veil of poetic beauty, appealing to the fancy rather than to the physical senses covers everything. Shakespeare himself intended his play to be regarded from the point of view of a dream, as is evident, not only from the various references to his own art and to the power of imagination, but also from Puck's apologetic speech, which stands in the place of an epilogue at the end of the play.

Question 4.

What is a masque? How does *A Midsummer Night's Dream* resemble a masque?

Answer

Masques were elaborate entertainments, presented for some special occasion, such as a marriage, and usually performed by distinguished amateurs, such as princes or other nobility. These presentations were written, usually, in rhymed verse and they included dialogue, singing and dancing. The characters in Ben Jonson's masques were usually mythological, though fairies also appear in at least one of them, and expensive movable scenery was used for them. The entertainment was often varied by what Jonson called antimasques—that is, parodies of the main masque, which were very humorous. The antimasque was sometimes designed to illustrate or parody the story of the main masque.

A Midsummer Night's Dream resembles a masque (1) in its general lyrical character and in the introduction of music and dances; (2) in the use of classical and mythological names and allusions; (3) in the sense that it has been produced for some special occasion; and (4) in the use of the farcical interlude or antimasque. The play differs from a masque (1) in that it is much longer than masques in general; (2) it is more dramatic and full of human interest; (3) it contains blank verse, whereas Ben Jonson's masques contain a great deal of prose; (4) the masques contain very elaborate and precise stage directions, sometimes occupying almost as much space as the play itself, and this is not the case with Shakespeare's play.

Question 5.

Why did Shakespeare place the interlude in the last act?

Answer

A Midsummer Night's Dream resembles a masque, produced probably for some special occasion. We have already seen that one of the ordinary features of a masque was an antimasque, designed to illustrate or parody the main story. The interlude of

Pyramus and Thisbe serves this purpose. Delicate, imaginative poetry is replaced by clumsiness and stupidity. Fairies are replaced by crude "mechanicals," blank verse by prose and love is made to look ridiculous by the hero and heroine of the piece.

Shakespeare also introduces the interlude in order to fulfil a promise made in the first scene of the play. The opening scene is of great importance in striking the keynote of a play. (Compare the opening scenes of *Macbeth* and *The Merchant of Venice*.) In the opening scene of this play, Theseus reveals some weariness and a desire to hurry the passage of time, "to ease the anguish of a torturing hour" he says, by witnessing some show.

> Go, Philostrate,
> Stir up th' Athenian youth to merriments;
> Awake the pert and nimble spirit of mirth.

Philostrate does as he is told, and the interlude is the result.

We may describe Shakespeare's purpose in another way. We know that he was a master of the technique of the dramatic art and that he used many different devices to maintain the interest of his audience: mistaken identities, disguises, misunderstandings, surprising adventures, the supernatural and practical jokes. In order to hold the attention of his public, he often introduced a secondary plot or a new phase of the main theme. He does this here. In the play, Shakespeare frequently refers to the power of imagination. It is a play of fancy. Puck, in the epilogue, describes the play as a dream and the characters in it as shadows. By introducing the unimaginative Athenian craftsmen, Shakespeare uses the dramatic device of contrast and, at the same time, gives Theseus an opportunity to comment on the necessity of imagination, not only in the presentation of a play, but also in an audience's appreciation of it.

However, the chief purpose of this comic interlude, coming after so much exquisite poetry, is, simply, to serve as comic relief and to make the audience laugh.

Question 6.
Suggest dramatic purposes served by the interlude?

Answer
The purposes are: (1) It provides humor in both its prepara-

tion and its performance; (2) It illustrates the customs of the day in providing entertainment by humble subjects on the occasion of the marriage of their lords; (3) It provides for the complication of Bottom and Titania; (4) It is an antimasque or parody on the love story of the four Athenian lovers; (5) Its ridiculous construction satirizes earlier tragedies offered to the public.

Question 7.
What evidence is there that Quince wrote the interlude?

Answer
The play nowhere states that Quince wrote the interlude, but there is sufficient evidence to allow us to assume that it is his composition. (1) Bottom tells us that Quince is a poet when he proposes to have him write a ballad about his dream; (2) The play selected by Quince and the parts assigned differ from those presented; (3) The prologue, which contains the names of the players and describes them, can apply only to this particular play; (4) In the original play, Lion is to do nothing but roar, but a speech is now assigned to him; a similar innovation occurs in the speeches of Moonshine and Wall; (5) The extreme absurdities of meter, rhyming, alliteration, padded lines, repetitions and exclamations point to an unskilled writer.

Question 8.
Identify and discuss the theme of the play.

Answer
The theme of *A Midsummer Night's Dream* is that "love hath no law but his own," that it is blind, unreasonable and unpredictable and that "all's fair in love and war." But, since the play is an entertaining fantasy, neither realistic nor tragic, we must not take its romantic moments too seriously. In fact, they are themselves made fun of, reflected in the distorting mirror of farce.

Practically everything that is said and done in the play, whether by the dignified Theseus and Hippolyta, the mixed-up young lovers, the fanciful, delicate fairies or the low comedians is related to this theme, so that the whole is a network of related threads that somehow form a satisfying pattern. If we think of the parts separately, it is like a piece of music in which a single movement is repeated in different keys and tempos.

Theseus, though he loves Hippolyta and will marry her, has won her love by defeating her in war. Hermia, for love of Lysander, defies her father and Athenian law. Demetrius claims to love Helena and then Hermia. Hermia, pursued by two young men, who, in the eyes of the world, are indistinguishably handsome, rich, and wellborn, adores one and hardly knows that the other exists. Demetrius, who has courted Helena and eventually marries her, hates her for a time and rejects her. She, for a few hours of his company, reveals the secret of her dearest friend.

We are not told whether the workmen have wives or sweethearts. But they are obsessed by the dream of moving an audience with a tragedy on the theme of obsessive love.

Oberon and Titania, though they are lord and lady and eventually settle their differences, are jealous of each other over Oberon's affairs with nymphs and Hippolyta and over Titania's doting on Theseus. Titania, though Oberon is her lord, has a priestess of her own and cherishes the priestess' boy; Oberon, though Titania is his lady, uses his magic to get the boy from her. Their quarrel is reflected in the unseasonable weather on earth and in the young lovers' quarrel, which follows the transfer of Lysander's affection. Titania's melting fondness for Bottom mirrors, in ridiculous fashion, the loves of Hermia and Helena and of all mortals who give affection to unworthy objects. Only the stability of the mature and noble duke, who does not believe in fairies and distrusts the excessive emotions of lovers almost as much as those of lunatics and poets, introduces order into the pattern and sets everything straight in the end. The interlude, a parody of love tragedies like *Romeo and Juliet*, is ridiculed for unskilled performance, but it is approved of in principle.

Question 9.
Discuss how the theme of change and transformation is present in this play.

Answer
There are many references to the theme of change and transformation, climaxing in Bottom's transformation and the change in the lovers' and in Titania's perception. The interlude also concerns the theme of change, for art transforms reality. Notice that the quarrel between Oberon and Titania is over a "changeling."

It is the king's desire to have this boy that is the moving force behind the plot. Not only the cause, but the result, of the quarrel concerns change: Titania explains that the seasons have become all turned around as a result of the disorders in their royal household. Cause, result, and now solution concern change, for the solution of the quarrel is possible because of a change in a "little western flower" (a pansy). The power of this changed flower is to change people's eyesight so that the first creature they look upon immediately after the juice of the flower is applied is transformed into their beloved.

The moon, which presides over the whole play, is constantly changing from one phase to another. Both love and art look to the moon as their guiding star, for both concern illusion and change. Art transforms reality, and we have been told over and over that love has to do, not with constancy, but with change.

Question 10.
Discuss the kinds of unreality presented in the play.

Answer
The play is a fantasy, and its unreality is of several different kinds. The very title warns us that it is all a dream, and that is the impression the young lovers and Bottom retain at the end. But just as Quince and his company put on a play within a play, so Hermia, Titania and Bottom have a dream within a dream.

Another unreality is that of time and place: these events all happened a long time ago, in a mythical city ruled by a mythical duke and his equally mythical bride. The young lovers and the actors are closer to reality, yet we know, even while we are laughing at them, that never on earth have there been couples quite so foolish and so confused or comedians so comically clumsy. Moreover, both these groups are touched by the supernatural world of the fairies, in whom we do not believe these days.

But to say that the play is a fantasy is not to say that it has no meaning. The characters, under the influence of magic and dreams, do nothing that is actually impossible in life.

Question 11.
Discuss Shakespeare's use of varied settings in *A Midsummer Night's Dream*.

Answer

The setting of *A Midsummer Night's Dream* is that of a masque, the stately forerunner of our musical comedy privately staged at some great house or palace at fabulous expense. Dancing, singing, elaborate costume and spectacle were the elements of the masque. It also readily allowed for the introduction of the supernatural and of clowning. Since the public playhouses of his time were financially unable to compete with private entertainments in scenes and costumes, Shakespeare supplied a setting of lovely poetic descriptions: the wood, with its flowers and lively, colorful creatures; the yellow sands and spiced Indian air, where Titania and her playful priestess watched the ships; Titania's bower; the mountain top from which, on a May morning, Theseus and his followers see the hunt and listen to the barking of the hounds in the valley below; the pomp and ceremony of Theseus' palace; and the haunted night in which the fairies bless the sleeping house.

Question 12.

Is the time scheme of the play clearly defined and accurate?

Answer

The references to night, day and time in general in the course of the action are frequently inconsistent when examined carefully, though the impressions of passing time and of continuity are rarely, if ever, lacking for the audience during a performance. Theseus says (Act I, Scene 1, 2) that four days and four nights will precede the wedding, which should, therefore, occur on the fifth day. But Hermia and Lysander (Act I, Scene 1, 164) and the actors (Act 1, Scene 2, 105-6) agree to meet "tomorrow night," so that Act II, Act III and part of Act IV occupy the second day and night. In Act IV, Scene 1, 97, we learn that this, the third day, is the wedding day. In the afternoon, Bottom rejoins his fellows (Act IV, Scene 2), and Act V takes place that evening. The moon is a stage moon, and, despite Bottom's insistence that they consult the almanac to "find out moonshine" (Act III, Scene 1, 53-55), no correspondence to the correct phase of the moon is to be expected.

Question 13.

Describe the character of Theseus.

Answer

Shakespeare's Theseus is really a romantic, rather than a classical character. As duke of Athens, he is somewhat like Henry V, king of England. He appears to be Shakespeare's earlier conception of his ideal king. Like King Henry, Theseus is a great warrior and a ruler who possesses dignity and majesty. He also bears some resemblance to the English king in the fact that his youth had been rather wild (Act II, Scene 1, 76-81). But that was when he was still under the influence of the fairies, an influence that faded before the period of his life presented in the play. Here we see him as a soldier and a man of action, who captured his wife with his sword, "won her love doing her injuries" and who, in times of peace, loved to hear the music of his hounds. His career has been one of conquest (Act V, Scene 1, 51, 93-100), and his triumphs have been celebrated in speeches prepared by great scholars, who have "shivered and looked pale" in the presence of so famous a soldier. But, being a man of action rather than of words, he could appreciate any service done for him "when simpleness and duty tender it." He has a preference for "the modesty of fearful duty," rather than for "The rattling tongue/Of saucy and audacious eloquence."

His love for Hippolyta is no romantic passion like the loves of his young Athenian subjects. Indeed, although he makes love at the beginning of the play in a dignified and stately fashion, we find him later comparing "the lunatic, the lover and the poet," apparently without any idea of including himself in his description (Act V, Scene 1, 7-20). He is certainly not unimaginative, but he keeps his imagination well under control and, thus, he differs from those who "are of imagination all compact." He cannot believe in the visions and dreams of the lovers in the forest, in "these antique fables, nor these fairy toys." His life has been too full of action and hard work to allow him to let his imagination run wild, but he has a very true idea of "the pleasures of the imagination." Unlike Hippolyta, to whom the interlude is simply "the silliest stuff that ever I heard," he can find enjoyment in the honest attempts of bumbling actors. He can "piece out their imperfections with his thoughts." To him, "the best in this kind are but shadows and the worst are no worse if imagination amend them."

Theseus is kind and generous and shows a strong desire to make everyone happy in his kingdom. He proclaims a holiday on the occasion of his marriage. He attempts to persuade Hermia to obey her father's will. Being a ruler, he naturally upholds the Athenian law, yet we feel all the time that his sympathies are with the daughter, rather than with the stern parent. When Demetrius expresses his determination to be true to his first love, the duke unhesitatingly overrules the will of Egeus. During the interlude, he apologizes for the imperfections of the actors, takes in very good humor the amusing corrections of Bottom (Act V, Scene 1, 184-7 and 354-5) and assures the players that it is "a fine tragedy, and very notably discharged."

Shakespeare was not concerned with depicting the character of Theseus as an Athenian ruler of a pagan age. Rather, he has really painted the picture of a contemporary English hunting nobleman. His pleasure is to go

> Up to the mountain's top,
> And mark the musical confusion
> Of hounds and echo in conjunction,
> (Act IV, Scene 1, 110)

and he has chosen a wife who shares his own tastes. His pride is in his "flew'd and sanded" hounds, "bred out of the Spartan kind." When he cannot be hunting, he requires some other "sport" (Act V, Scene 1, 42, 90) with which "to ease the anguish of a torturing hour."

Question 14.
Describe Hippolyta's limited role in the play.

Answer
She is mainly a silent actor in the play. She takes her place with dignity as a soldier queen by the side of her soldier husband-to-be. She is patient (Act I, Scene 1, 7-11), yet she often addresses her future lord in affectionate terms. It is difficult to imagine her ever having had a very close connection with the fairy world, although Titania speaks of her to Oberon as "your buskin'd mistress, and your warrior love." The remarks she makes during the performance of the interlude—"This is the silliest stuff that ever I heard," "I am aweary of this moon; would he would change," "such a Pyramus" and "I hope she will be brief"—do not tend to encourage the actors. But we may, perhaps, excuse her rudeness,

remembering that she has been, until now, a stranger to the civilization of Athens.

Question 15.
Trace the development of Hermia's character.

Answer
At first, Hermia is the typical young girl in love against her father's wishes. We have a slight clue that a real person lies behind this conventional exterior when she promises to meet Lysander "By all the vows that ever men have broke/In number more than ever women spoke." This remark has life and reality, especially in the light of what follows. This remark also shows a spark of originality (she could have just sworn on her life the way Lysander is always doing). When the play has progressed to the height of love's confusion, Hermia's character becomes very distinct. She is dark and small, but quick-tempered and even fierce. Though she and Helena may once have been girlish companions, under the pressure of love and its frustrations, this friendship is destroyed, and each girl emerges as a separate personality. Driven almost to madness by Lysander's unaccountable rejection of her, Hermia asks, "Am not I Hermia? are not you Lysander?"

The men, who are not in control of the situation at all, keep insisting upon their new-found sanity and seriousness. But Hermia, who remains constant throughout, sees her very identity at stake. Her awareness of this question is itself an assertion of her identity, so that, when she gets her Lysander back, she gets more than just that. She gets herself back too by having felt the basis of her identity threatened. Hermia does not say anything during the performance of the play. In fact, her last words are in Act IV, Scene 1, when she says she feels as if she were seeing double. Perhaps Hermia's silence in the rest of the play indicates that the experience she had in the woods did have a permanent, beneficial effect.

Question 16.
Sketch the character of Helena.

Answer
Helena is the lovesick maiden. She is tall and fair and, until events in the forest change the affections of Lysander and Deme-

trius, she mourns pitifully over her cruel beloved. She does show some initiative when she betrays her best friend so that she can gain her own ends with her boyfriend.

Her persistent humility is certainly remarkable. When she suddenly finds herself loved by two instead of by none, she is forced out of her accustomed role. She is full of self-pity at this discomfort—she's much more accustomed to being rejected through long habit. Her immediate reaction is to suspect a plot, and she pities herself all the more. Her chief defence is that her situation deserves pity, not scorn. This attitude remains intact for a time. She uses it artfully to shame Hermia, saying that the latter betrays their long friendship. How can Hermia be so cruel to such a sweet, dear, faithful, trusting friend, one who has had such a hard time already?

Helena finally confesses that she betrayed her friend's confidence and told the person who would most like to spoil the elopement all about it. A little later, it is revealed by the frightened Helena that things weren't so rosy back in the good old days either. In fact, Helena's opinion is that Hermia was fierce and quarrelsome at school.

Under pressure, Helena ventures out a little more on her own too. She actually gathers her drooping, lovesick self together enough to run away from Hermia. Fear of bodily harm from her little friend replaces the sorrow with which she endured all threats from Demetrius. This abandonment of her initial role is a step forward toward an individual personality. Running from Hermia interests us much more than her running after Demetrius. Helena, too, says no more after Act IV, Scene 1, and her comment there is quite perceptive. She says she can't feel secure about Demetrius— it's like finding a jewel by lucky accident. Somehow, Helena knows what she's getting when she gets Demetrius.

Question 17.
Compare the physical appearance of Hermia and Helena.

Answer
The two ladies are equally beautiful. They are "two lovely berries moulded on one stem," and Helena is, throughout Athens, considered as fair as Hermia. But, although we may not say that one is more beautiful than the other, we are able to distinguish in them two different types of beauty. Hermia's

beauty is the gipsy type; hence, she is scornfully described as an "Ethiope," an "acorn," a "raven," and "a tawny Tartar." Helena is fair, and her pink and white complexion wins from Hermia the spiteful description of "painted maypole." Hermia is short, a "puppet" in height, while Helena is taller.

Question 18.

Compare and contrast the characters of Demetrius and Lysander.

Answer

The two men are alike in that they are wellborn, wealthy, young, ready to assert their rights with the sword and in love.

Lysander is faithful in love, except when under the influence of Puck's charm. Demetrius is unfaithful to Helena after becoming engaged to her, for no apparent reason, but he returns to her after Puck interferes. Lysander is romantic, singing ballads under Hermia's window and making her gifts of sentimental value. Demetrius is aggressive in demanding Lysander's surrender of his claims to Hermia in the presence of the duke, threatening to make him end his interest in Helena in the woods, and challenging him to fight. Lysander becomes angry only when Hermia stops him from fighting, while Demetrius is always inclined to be hot-tempered and sharp-tongued.

Question 19.

Describe the character of Egeus.

Answer

The father of Hermia, Egeus, is the typical dissatisfied father, whose daughter is silly enough to love whom she wants, not whom he wants. The first words we hear him speak establish him as this kind of character. He says he's "full of vexation" at Hermia, and the reasons he gives are the typical response of the older generation to young and foolish love. Egeus is a man to whom the beauties of love are just nonsense. Balconies by moonlight, love poetry, souvenirs, gifts of jewelry and candy are all a silly nuisance in his opinion. All they do is interfere with the orderly, businesslike fulfilment by a dutiful daughter of a marriage contract made by a responsible father. Egeus represents this classical attitude toward love and marriage. He would rather see his daughter dead or shut up in a nunnery than married to someone he hasn't chosen for her.

Question 20.
Sketch the character of Nick Bottom.

Answer
Nick Bottom, the weaver, is one of Shakespeare's most memorable creations. When we first meet him, *Pyramus and Thisbe* is being cast. Bottom is ready to take on anything. He has complete confidence in his ability to sweep from one end of the emotional scale to the other. The energy and enthusiasm with which he participates in life are immediately evident. Some critics have objected to what they consider his domineering, loud, self-centered personality, but this is a gross misunderstanding. When he shares Titania's bower, his graciousness with his extraordinary new companions is an indication of his remarkable ability to adapt immediately to whatever life offers him. His energetic love of life, his naïveté and eager innocence allow him to enter this other world, so different from his own. And he enjoys it to the fullest. When Bottom awakens from his "dream," his own manner of reacting to it is the best approach to the experience. Wonder, awe and a strong sense of the power beyond man's understanding are expressed by him. He rightly declares the incredibility of his "dream" and feels most profoundly its power. He knows that it should be called "Bottom's Dream" for these reasons. Starting from his position as a realist, Bottom can, with the same vigor and joy he brings to whatever he does, respond to this power and believe.

The fantastically transformed Bottom becomes a participator in the fairy world in the incredible role of Titania's lover. He conducts himself with such seriousness and such grace, with his own good sense and yet with such enjoyment that we see he is supremely capable of uniting these separate worlds. He represents the union of reality and illusion. His love of life enables him to play his double role in it to the fullest. In this play, where love and art and dreams assert their power over life, Bottom stands for the merging of reality and illusion.

Question 21.
Describe the fairies in *A Midsummer Night's Dream*.

Answer

They are extremely tiny creatures. They can "creep into acorn cups and hide them there" (Act II, Scene 1, 31); the "enamelled skin" shed by a snake is "weed wide enough to wrap a fairy in" (Act II, Scene 1, 256); and they "war with reremice for their leathern wings" (Act II, Scene 2, 4) to make coats for their small elves. Their dainty and delicate nature is further suggested by their names—Peaseblossom, Cobweb, Moth and Mustardseed.

They possess the power of moving from one place to another with extreme swiftness. They can "wander everywhere, swifter than the moon's sphere." (Act II, Scene 1, 7) Puck can "put a girdle round the world in forty minutes" (Act II, Scene 1, 176); he can fly "swifter than the wind" (Act III, Scene 2, 94) or than "arrow from the Tartar's bow." (Act III, Scene 2, 101) They can make themselves invisible to mortals (Act II, Scene 1, 187) and can "overcast the night" (Act III, Scene 2, 357). When they quarrel, all nature is disturbed (Act II, Scene 1, 116-8). But their special function is to confer blessings and prevent disaster (Act V, Scene 1, 403-25).

Question 22.

How does Shakespeare succeed in making the fairies seem both real and fanciful at the same time?

Answer

By giving them their tiny size, fairy names, an interest in song, dance and flowers, control of the elements, independence of time and space, night habits, mysterious interference in human affairs, irresponsibility and indifference to ordinary emotions, he provides them with supernatural or visionary qualities. But, by the stage necessity of beings of human size playing their parts, by endowing Oberon and Titania with such unflattering and petty qualities as jealousy, envy (over the page), bad tempers (causing unreasonable weather) and ridicule (in the incident of Titania and Bottom), they appear similar to human beings.

Question 23.

Shakespeare emphasizes the fickleness of love in human beings by showing that the fairies, who have such power over men and women, are also inconstant in love. Discuss this statement.

Answer

Fickleness in love appears only in Demetrius and Lysander, for Hermia and Helena remain constant, as do Theseus and Hippolyta. But, since the main story deals with the four lovers, the rapid changes in their love become very important.

The fairies not only interfere with the lovers, but they represent their romantic and idealistic hopes, and, therefore, it is suitable that they should also have the same quality of fickleness. Titania and Oberon each accuse the other of earlier loves, and she charges him with coming to the wedding because of his interest in Hippolyta. Then, Oberon deliberately makes her fall in love with the first creature she sees. She falls madly in love with Bottom, and, when her ridiculous romance is pointed out to her, it is passed over lightly by both her and her husband.

Question 24.

Describe the nature and habits of Puck.

Answer

Puck, the "merry wanderer of the night," stands in a class by himself. He acts as Oberon's assistant and performs his errands sometimes well and sometimes not. But when Puck does wrong, he feels no regret. In fact, he rejoices when his ill-doing works mischief among the mortals he loves to torment.

His love of mischief and his natural disposition for tricks make him the jester in the court of King Oberon, who treats him like a spoiled child. He is recognized as a "lob of spirits" by Titania's fairy, who knows him as a "shrewd and knavish sprite called Robin Goodfellow," who loves to frighten village maidens, mislead night wanderers,

And bootless make the breathless housewife churn;
And sometime make the drink to bear no barm.

He has a preference for what is attractive and clean over what is ugly or foul, but he always acts without any reference to principles of right and wrong. He is skilful in all transformations and can turn himself into a horse, a hound, a hog, a headless bear or a fire:

And neigh, and bark, and grunt, and roar, and burn,
Like horse, hound, hog, bear, fire, at every turn.

The "jangling" of mortals is, to him, a sport, and the embarrassment of lovers a "fond pageant," for those things "that befall preposterously" please him most. He appreciates flattery and will even work for "those that Hobgoblin call him and sweet Puck." He pities the beautiful Hermia in distress, and the sight of Helena, "curst and sad," makes him forget, for a moment, his own mischief as he considers that of the god, Cupid. He assures us, at the close of the play, that he is "an honest Puck," but there is certainly nothing in his actions that would lead us to accept this view of him.

Question 25.
Sketch the character of Oberon.

Answer
The king of the fairies has the majesty and power in his world that Theseus has in his. The difference between the two worlds reflects the difference between the two characters. Oberon is a master of poetry and illusion—"King of Shadows," Puck calls him—while, as mere shadows, Theseus scorns even the most expert creators of illusion (Act V, Scene 1, 212-213). The marriage of Theseus is the framing event in the daylight world of the play. It is the first thing we hear of and the last thing that happens, but the cloth that is woven within this frame is of Oberon's design. He and his assistant, Puck, move the shuttle of this loom between the straight uprights of Theseus' frame.

All this comes about because Oberon can't have something that he wants. Titania has a changeling, whom she has excellent reasons for wishing to keep. The little boy's mother was a special friend who died giving birth to this child. But Oberon must have this boy. He obtains the love juice to divert Titania's interest from the child and he'll only disenchant her once the changeling is securely his own. When we remember that this is the motive behind all that happens in the woods, Oberon seems as petty as the two male lovers. In generosity of spirit and depth of emotion, he's about on a par with them. However, as soon as Oberon speaks the poetry Shakespeare has given him, we, too, are completely in his power. His magnificent description of the occasion when he first saw "the little western flower" overcomes any lingering doubts about the petty purpose he intends it for. His poetry creates a music that made "the rude sea" grow civilized and caused the stars to shoot "madly from their spheres." This is the Oberon we remember, the "King of Shadows," to whom such things happen and who can thus recreate his experiences.

Question 26.
What part does Titania take in the play?

Answer
The play is one in which the theme of love is lightly treated. The love of the mortals does not represent an enduring or profound sentiment, but is represented as being the effect of some visual enchantment, which it is in the power of the king of the fairies to inspire. Such love is seen in its simplest form in Titania. She loves everything that is beautiful, but with no deep feeling. She delights in the pretty swimming movements of her mortal friend and in the lovely boy to whom her friend gave birth. She is attracted by flowers and dewdrops, birds and painted butterflies and seeks only festivities and pleasures. There is jealousy between herself and Oberon, but there is no trace of a reflection, no indication of feeling when she awakens from her vision and says, "Methought I was enamoured of an ass," adding, "O how mine eyes do loathe his visage now!" She is only affected by the idea of the actual and the visible. In depicting her as being infatuated with Bottom, wearing the features of a hairy ass, Shakespeare has painted a pathetic and irresistibly comic picture. She "Crowns him with flowers, and makes him all her joy," just as she had formerly petted her sweet changeling boy. The playwright has shown us something of the comedy of love. We may feel pity for her "dotage," as Oberon did when he saw her:

> Seeking sweet favours for this hateful fool,
> But our pity will only be a transient feeling, as fleeting
> As that same dew, which sometime on the buds
> Was wont to swell like round and orient pearls.

and which
> Stood now within the pretty flowerets' eyes,
> Like tears that did their own disgrace bewail,

for we know that her infatuation cannot be lasting and that it will leave no deeper impression upon her than "the fierce vexation of a dream."

Question 27.

Discuss the use of song and dance in *A Midsummer Night's Dream*.

Answer

Song is indicated in the stage directions only three times: the first time, when the fairies sing Titania to sleep before Oberon anoints her eyes; the second time, when Bottom awakens her; and the third time, as they all bless the newly married couples. But many of the play's poetic meters may easily be put to song. Special music is called for several times. The movements of the attendant fairies and Puck are always in dance. Oberon and Titania dance together after their reconciliation and, again, in their closing performance in the palace. The rowdy and clumsy dance or "bergomask" of the two clowns after the play is a parody of the dance of the fairies and may be made very amusing in its contrast.

Question 28.

How does Shakespeare vary his verse according to the character of the speaker or the nature of the subject being discussed?

Answer

The fairies usually speak in rhymed verse, appropriate to delicate and poetic beings, but they use blank verse when they quarrel. (Act II, Scene 1, 60) In Act III, Scene 1, 155-160, we have a series of six rhyming lines repeating a single sound, perhaps to mark the very strong contrast between the poetry of Titania and the crudeness of Bottom. *A Midsummer Night's Dream* being one of Shakespeare's earlier plays, the changes of meter, which are designed to produce an emotional effect, are not so numerous as in some later plays. The following points, however, are worthy of consideration. Act I, Scene 1, is in blank verse as far as line 171. Lines 171-8 contain the expression of a single thought and are in rhyme. Before line 171, the conversation had been more or less businesslike, but the entrance of Helena gives rise to a more emotional theme, which is expressed in rhyme. Soliloquies, the quiet expression of thought, are usually in rhymed verse, as at the end of Act I, Scene 1 and Act II, Scene 2. In the latter case, Hermia's excitement is indicated by the irregularity of the accent. These passages may be contrasted with the speeches of Theseus at the beginning of Act V. Here, the comparative frequency with which the unaccented ending occurs distinguishes the wise philosophy of Theseus from the more romantic and poetical character of the speeches of the others and at the same time reproduces, to some extent, the easy tone of ordinary life. Notice, again, the change from rhyme to blank verse in Act III, Scene 2, 194, marking the excitement of the speakers, still further indicated by the number of unstressed endings, increasing with their growing passion.

Question 29.

Comment on the major motifs and images in the play.

Answer

The use of one's eyes in love is introduced right at the beginning of the play, when Theseus tries to convince Hermia to obey her father. The disobedient daughter says she wishes her father saw with her eyes. The duke replies that her eyes ought to be governed by his judgment. When Oberon steps into the picture with his love juice, we see that linking judgment to vision in matters of love is not as straightforward as Theseus thinks it is. When Helena speaks of how the blind, winged boy, Cupid, is the appropriate god of love, she, too, brings up the question of using one's eyes in love. This motif comes to a climax when Oberon and Puck apply the magic juice to Titania, Lysander and Demetrius. The charm is specifically directed at the eyes, and, under its spell, a person looks and loves instantly. Judgment, reason and will are all of no account whatsoever.

When the confused males protest that judgment, reason and will form the basis of their love, comedy is the result. After awakening from their enchanted experiences, Bottom and the lovers speak of what has happened in terms of eyesight. Demetrius says it's like trying to distinguish a landscape at a very great distance; Hermia feels as though she's seeing double; Helena can't believe her eyes. Bottom speaks of having had a "most rare vision." However, he expands the meaning of "vision" when he says that his vision passes beyond the evidence of all the senses.

Flowers enter into the scene of this play frequently. The fairy world that Shakespeare has created in this play is characterized, in part, by its association with flowers. In the scene where we first meet the fairies, nine flowers are mentioned. They continue to be mentioned throughout, and, of course, the love charm is contained in the juice of a flower. The duke's famous speech about "single blessedness" uses a flower to dramatize the argument.

The moon is a real presence in this play. It is mentioned many times, and its light bathes the action of the play. At the very beginning of the play, it is used by the duke and his intended bride to measure the time until their wedding. The lovers make plans to meet by moonlight and elope. The workmen also plan to meet by moonlight in order to rehearse their play in privacy. The moon is important to this last group in the further sense that they must have it in their play. Down-to-earth as they are, they have one of their own company represent Moonshine, rather than leave the matter up to the moon itself. In short, the moon presides over the night, and it is "night-rule" that creates chaos.

Question 30.
Comment briefly on the element of fate in the play.

Answer
Fate is a power greater than fairydom. Puck blames its interference for his mistake in applying the love potion to the wrong Athenian's eyes and, at the same time, he hypocritically accuses it of interfering in the affairs of mortals. Hermia accepts the duke's decision against her marriage to Lysander as a decree of fate, until Lysander takes matters in his own hands and overcomes it. Apart from these instances, fate figures little in the play. Puck's finding the clowns at their rehearsal in the wood, a coincidence which delivered Bottom into his hands, is rather indicative of his presence everywhere, rather than the overwhelming power and presence of fate.

Question 31.
Illustrate from the play Shakespeare's use of nature.

Answer
Shakespeare's observation of nature was that of a poet and an artist, rather than that of a naturalist. His accuracy and knowl-

edge were remarkable in an age when little attention was paid to botany or to natural history. His keen awareness of nature is evident, not only in his close observation of animals and habits and in his intimate acquaintance with all varieties of flowers and their characteristics, but, above all, in his imagery and in his descriptive expressions. The poet's knowledge of country life may be said to pervade the whole of *A Midsummer Night's Dream*. Not only is it exhibited in descriptive passages, but images faithfully copied from nature and accurately represented in words are blended with personal descriptions in the most dramatic passages.

Notice how Shakespeare, by metaphors and figures of speech, condenses into single lines a vast sense of past and possible experiences:

But earthlier happy is the rose distill'd
(Act I, Scene 1, 76)

Your tongue's sweet air
More tuneable than lark to shepherd's ear
When wheat is green, when hawthorn buds appear.
(Act I, Scene 1, 183)

Two lovely berries moulded on one stem.
(Act III, Scene 2, 211)

You minimus of hindering knot-grass made.
(Act III, Scene 2, 331)

Observe again, the delicate poetry and the vivid colors in the following:

[Phoebe] decking with liquid pearl the bladed grass.
(Act I, Scene 1, 211)

Even till the eastern gate, all fiery-red,
Opening on Neptune with fair blessed beams,
Turns into yellow gold his salt-green streams.
(Act III, Scene 2, 393)

Oberon's picture of Titania's bower, "I know a bank where the wild thyme blows," is also picturesque.

Shakespeare's mastery of descriptive expressions is apparent in the following examples: "Faint primrose beds," "the cowslips tall," "the nodding violet," "weaving spiders," "long legg'd spinners," "plain-song cuckoo," "russet-pated choughs" and "red-hipped humble bee on the top of a thistle."

The accuracy and precision with which the sound of a pack of hounds is described is remarkable in the line, "Match'd in mouth like bells, each under each." In this passage, much knowledge and observation are conveyed in few words.

NOTES

NOTES

NOTES

NOTES

NOTES

NOTES

NOTES

NOTES

NOTES

NOTES

NOTES

NOTES

NOTES

NOTES

Don't forget to match that tough textbook with helpful
COLES NOTES

Expertly written, fast review summaries designed to give a greater understanding of the subject.

1984
Odyssey
Of Mice and Men
Old Man and the Sea
Oliver Twist
One Flew Over the Cuckoo's Nest
Paradise Lost
Passage to India
Pearl
Persuasion
Pickwick Papers
Pilgrim's Progress

Portrait of the Artist as a Young Man
Power and the Glory
Pride and Prejudice
Prince-Machiavelli
Pygmalion
Rape of the Lock
Saint Joan
Scarlet Letter
Separate Peace
Sons and Lovers
Stone Angel and Other Works
Stranger, Plague
Streetcar Named Desire
Such is My Beloved, More Joy in Heaven
Sun Also Rises, Snows of Kilimanjaro

Surfacing
Tale of Two Cities
Tess of the D'Ubervilles
To Kill a Mockingbird
Tom Jones
Two Solitudes
Ulysses
Vanity Fair
Waiting for Godot
War and Peace
Who Has Seen the Wind
Wordsworth's Poetry Notes
Works of John Donne
Wuthering Heights
Yeats' Poetry Notes